The Path of Grief

and the Imagined Future

Piper Winifred, PhD

Table of Contents

Dear Reader:

I imagine us sitting around the kitchen table, talking. Maybe we are at a cozy coffee shop, chatting on comfortable couches pulled up around a welcoming fireplace. However the imagination takes hold, I picture us sharing our experiences together. Grief, mourning, pain, and loss: these are the component pieces of the Journey we are about to undertake. They are also inevitable facets—or twists and turns of the Path that is Life, and yet we too often endure them alone. It is so true that this part of our Journey is unique and individual, but I believe we also need to share our burdens. Together, we can find a way to accept the changes that have come our way. I offer my hand to hold, by sharing my thoughts in the hope that my words nudge your memories and allow the healing process to begin or continue. As we sit around the fire, or at the kitchen table, or wherever/however we may find ourselves, let us seek the solace and comfort that community offers.

In a way, it took me four years to write this book. In the beginning, I had no idea of this being a book about Grief. My daily journal and meditations became a series of entries: a particular sort of journey, leading to this work.

Somewhere or somewhen along the way, I discovered that no specific words or phrases exist to describe the grieving process.

It is individual, mighty, quiet, complicated, and part of life. Although they exist, I was not thinking of "stages" while I mourned; I was living it and trying to find my path.

There are many reasons to grieve; it is part of the human condition in that pain and loss are part of life's journey. This is a book about death and the grief that surrounds it. Each person's pain is unique. There is nothing equal to coping with death through violence or crime, or the misery and confusion of suicide. The death of a longtime love or brand-new-what-might-have-been loved one or potential love each bring their own misery. The death of a child is almost incomprehensible. The death of a pet can be devastating, as well as a sibling or friend. Each carries its own particular anguish. Even the recognition of death is a horrific process. To be alive when death arrives is an affront.

In addition to all of this, each of us is a unique human being with our own valuable personality and way of coping or walking our path. We will be at different stages on the journey. I write as a daughter who lost her father to cancer, hoping to encapsulate the experience in a way that will embrace all of your experiences.

Grief is an inevitable part of the Path of Pain and Suffering that comes with loss. We typically associate this loss with the death of someone close to us or someone important in our life, but it can occur through any significant loss. Bereavement is complex.

While I write in these pages about the death of my father, I recognize that other painful losses and renderings in my life are present in my Journey. This is true for you, too.

I am sure that you, Dear Reader, have suffered too. You have felt the pain and sorrow that comes with loss or an injury so profound that you have lost something deep and essential to your Self. Sometimes the agony is accompanied by further harm, injury, and ongoing damage. The cost can be great.

It is difficult and exhausting to manage the thoughts and feelings that result. Time passes, but we often stay rooted in the torment. How do we move forward? How do we learn to live again in a way that is healthy and filled with purpose and meaning--even happiness?

I recognize that each of us has our individual burden and our unique story to tell. I offer mine to you in the hope that it [my story] offers markers along the Path to Recovery for you to insert YOUR story and find a way to a meaningful Imagined Future filled with Hope.

Somehow within the exploration of the way memories fit into the making of a relationship (the self with the loved one we lost and/or the self we lost due to circumstances that caused our grief) joined to the idea that I (we) can fashion an Imagined Future beyond the many facets of what grief is, there is an answer.

It seems to be common thought that there are five stages of grief, first identified by psychiatrist Elisabeth Kübler-Ross in her 1969 book <u>On Death and Dying</u>:

- Denial & Isolation
- Anger
- Bargaining
- Depression
- Acceptance

I would say that there is no set formula for grieving, and that each person finds and follows an individual course. The stages listed above are probably evident in my Journey, but they did not occur in any particular order and they often overlapped. I do not claim to have "the" answer.

What I know is that I lived it (and continue to wrestle with it), and because of that, I have a deeper understanding now, of what it means to truly grieve: to plunge into the abyss and plumb the depths of sorrow. I wrote from my heart and I offer my experience as one that is very human and filled with questions.

Please forgive me in advance for any (and every) boundary line(s) I cross as I attempt to describe the Path of Grief in the hope that I can offer my hand for you to hold, knowing in advance, that some of you do not want to hold ANY hand, but desire something else. I will try to offer that, too.

I offer my story to you, hoping that it touches you in profound ways and delicate places that will allow you to face your story and find your Path of Grief, the Journey that leads to your ideal, Imagined Future.

My goal has been to provide an authentic rendering of the course, with the hope that my experience resonates with you as you either recall your own struggle with grief, or as you face this same journey. I invite you to join me online and add your personal thoughts and reflections. Perhaps my journey will be one that parallels your own, and we can share the path.

All my very best wishes,

Piper Winifred
www.theimaginedfuture.com

"In the face of events that threaten to overwhelm our lives, storytelling gives us a way of reclaiming ourselves and reaffirming our connections with other people--those who listen to our stories and, by doing so, bear witness with us."

~ Victoria Alexander[1]

"Grief is a process of awareness, of making real inside the self an event that already occurred in reality outside."

~Parkes and Weiss[2]

Chapter 1: What is Time?

. . . and why has it stopped? Something feels different when death appears, and now life's Path—MY Life's Path—is reduced to slow motion. I am acutely aware of myself existing in time passing, and of my self in time. My mind reaches out to capture one solitary fragment, yet my focus is incomplete. In that instant of almost-present, the moment moves on.

Have you ever felt displaced or outside of life and living like this:

- Out of step
- Out of tune
- Outside of time
- Standing still

. . . while the world moves on?

I think mourning is like this. The grieving process places a miasma over the mourner as if the world has stopped turning and the sun no longer rises and sets. This is partly why grief is so significant and notice-able. I am often out of sync these days. Have you felt this, too?

How did this happen, and why can I not just "pull it together"?

Let us say that we can consider a sliver of time. If I stand in that fragment of awareness and gaze backwards at the path that brought me here . . .

- Can I see it?
- Can I feel it?
- Where does that path exist?

Life as a Path

Life has often been compared to a Journey. The course of that Journey is the individual Path each of us forms along the way. We form our Path by processing our:

- Thoughts
- Feelings
- Beliefs
- Actions
- Imagination
- Connections to others
- Memories and Reflections

These processes are part of what make us human beings, and together, they form the stepping stones of the Path: *Thinking, Feeling, Believing, Imagining, Acting, Connecting,* and *Reflecting.* Each of these practices can be either passive or active, can happen simultaneously, overlap, occur one at a time, and in any order. When I think, feel, believe, and act I determine where my Path leads. What I imagine will influence the direction of my future existence.

<u>Who</u> I connect with and <u>how</u> I process my memories will also have a defining impact on the Path.

The Path Represents Movement in Life or Time.

We each create our Path every day [indeed, every hour], and as we do, we visualize it in our "mind's eye." What does that mean? It means that in a way, we create our own Path, but this might not mean what we think it does. We do not create the world around us, but rather, we perceive it and then we process our perceptions. The manner in which we process those perceptions becomes our Path.

In reflection, when I reach back to my Stream of Memories, I better understand how I arrived at this particular point in Life and Time, and I find I need this giant pause right now. I might be able to change it! (Maybe I just want to understand it.) I ask myself not only "How did this happen?" but also, "What does this mean?"

In order to comprehend/understand/absorb . . . even acknowledge this bewildering Present-Time, how far back in Memory do I need to reach? Can I discern whether my memories come from my mind, or could they be twice-told tales, related to me while looking at scrapbooks and photo albums from childhood? Does my memory surround photographs and stories, or actual events? How do I determine what is real?

Does it matter?

Whichever it is, and however reliable, memories have brought me to this place and in this way to cold, harsh reality:

To the Eternal Present.
And my Dad is Dead.

The Seth Thomas clock on the mantle rings the hour, and it is a familiar sound, resonating through the years of my childhood and now, too, in present time. The clock that once was my grandmother's and then my father's, which now sits over my fireplace marks more than just the passing of hours and days. Present and past combine in an heirloom object that makes me take note every time I hear it toll, because it verifies reality.

> The clock on the mantle was my Gramma Bee's. . .
> Then my father's clock. . .
> And now it is mine.
> Can an object be a memory?
> The iconic status of time wrapped up in recollection.

> Do you have objects tied to memories and to the loved one or event you now mourn?
> Does it/do they provide a focus?
> Does this help?

One of the mind exercises I go through is a continual reflection of the question: "Who am I?" I mean, rather: "Who am I, *now*?" Am I suddenly somehow different now that grief has torn asunder what I thought was my life?

Can I define the self that is my True Self in the same way? Has my reason for living changed, or is that just a silly or melodramatic question I would never voice aloud?

What do I think of when I imagine my True Self? How about you? What do you think of when you imagine your True Self? Has that changed recently?

If I were to choose one medium by which to express existence, it would be seawater and ocean depths. The sea is ever present in my life as if it were a theme. It is background to all my lullabies, and the answer to where I want to go. I am a water baby at every age of life, and also afraid, sometimes, of the call and pull of the sea.

- Ebb and Flow.
- Tidal pull.

Standing in the *now* I face another direction, looking forward to the future. Where does the future exist? Not having happened yet, it exists in my imagination.

I imagine a voyage. I wonder if I will venture forth with companions, or if this is necessarily a solitary journey? It feels bleak and lonesome. I like to think I can imagine anything, but the death and dying of my father becomes something more than just a life event: something deeper and life changing.

The historical, iconic *Search for the Father* parallels the *Search for the Self* and becomes a Journey filled with unexpected tears and tender moments, challenges and new awakenings, plateaus and precipices, and mostly sailing into unchartered territory. The water is deep, and I learn what others before me have discovered: that life is filled with choices and growth.

Or not.

My Imagined Future is a choice--is my choice-- and it becomes a true statement to say that I can only GO where I can first imagine. Whatever and however we imagine, is where and how we will move forward (backward, or remain in place).

- What will I imagine and
- How will I imagine it?

Does this process involve <u>going</u> as in movement, and if so, how will I move with this stillness (stagnation?) that I feel?

What if thinking and imagining keep me marooned for a while—is that normal? Is it ok? Oh, and by the way, what is normal?

Does it matter?

How do these 'themes' of life operate—as twice told tales utilizing family photo albums, anecdotes, and oft-visited places?
Why are these memories—often-shared memories—so important in times of trial?
--I don't know, they just are.

There will always remain gaps in my father's life of which I am unaware: those places and events I will never and cannot know, yet somehow operate as themes.
This will eventually be the same for my children and me, as well as with my friends and me.
These are strange thoughts.

Can you identify a theme in your life?
--Something that holds together the essence of your Self?

Does everyone wrestle with these thoughts and imaginings upon the death of a loved one, or the end of a life's dream, or an abrupt life-altering outcome?

I think we wonder where we fit in the world: in the past when the loved one was still alive; before things broke or fell apart; when things were "normal" or "good". . . or at least "known"?

So how do we "go" there?
Given the memories of that former belonging,
how do we imagine life without that same sense of belonging no longer available to us?
Where will we go and be?

In time, I walk my Path while Time moves through me with all these thoughts swirling about, marking the Path ahead. For now, I feel only the numbness, while the clock keeps ticking without me.

I cannot tell you about Time, for I am out of sync.

"Let me come in when you are weeping, friend, and let me take your hand. I, who have known sorrow such as yours, can understand."

~*Grace Noll Crowell*[3]

Chapter 2: Ranting & Raving

When I was a growing up and well into my teen-age years, using the old rotary dial telephone attached to the kitchen wall to connect to Eastport, Maine meant going through the town's operator:

"Oh, it's little Piper!" she would announce to those who were present, and presumably they cared.

"How are you deah?" she would ask in that wonderful Down East accent.

After a few niceties, she would connect me to my Gramma Bee—WHEREVER she happened to be in town, because of course everyone knew everyone else's business. I miss that.

This year began with an abrupt acknowledgement of my father's mortality, when he was diagnosed with cancer. In one day, my father—my sister and I call him Doggy Daddy—went in to see the doctor healthy, and came out with a diagnosis of cancer. How did this happen? Daddies are not supposed to become less than; they just **are**.

He is far away in Eastport, Maine, and I am in Central Texas where there is no switchboard operator to tell me where he is at all hours of the day. In an age of cell phones, my father refuses to be that available. He has a daily routine, and those who know him know where to find him, but it requires physical presence or patience.

Although his art studio is also online and we can view his work-- his sculptures and pottery—via a website, he has only in the past year started using e-mail. He connects to the web at the local coffee shop with his laptop, and he jokingly refers to e-mail addresses as "call signs." I picture the twinkle in his eyes that matches his war stories about radioing HQ from the field, and I know he believes we are a primitive generation for replacing civilized letter writing and real conversation for the shortened half-sentences of the delayed messages that are e-mails.

Nevertheless, he has complied with his children's wishes for: "Please, Dad, we just want to hear your voice."

He raises his eyebrows, I know.

That man who lives so far away, a Dad who still feels oh-so-present and maybe even larger-than-life despite the decades apart and the roller coaster ride that is life . . .

. . . is that how fathers are?

When someone we love dies, we come face-to-face with the many worlds in which they lived. Those worlds seem so different because they are foreign to us, yet we also realize our loved one traversed them as if they encompassed ONE Journey and ONE path.
It was a single life, after all.

This is one of the "aha!" moments of grieving. It is in death that we are so clearly faced with the LIFE of another: an Other.

Perhaps when our beloved was alive, we thought of him or her in the context of our own experience.
In death, we are confronted with the individual, unique life as it was experienced.

It takes the breath away.
Or maybe just makes it hard to breathe?
How do I cope with the new knowledge of the entirety of my loved one's life that I never knew 'till now?
Do I miss only what I experienced and knew of before, or do I grieve for what I also never knew and never knew about?

Our Path is not solitary. We live in a human world with other human beings, each of whom formulate and move along paths of their own.

No two paths are the same, but they can be parallel, intersect occasionally, often overlap, connect somewhere in between, or never meet at all. Our paths might resemble each other or be completely dissimilar. In diverse ways and at different times, we connect:

- Link
- Bond
- Reach out
- Merge
- Join
- Simply notice

We connect with other people and their paths. This can be intentional or random, and sometimes we do not know that it has happened until afterwards, when we feel the loss. The connecting of paths, however, has an effect on both paths.

I think of my baby pictures, and of my baby self, standing on my father's outstretched palm as he lifted me to the ceiling or the sky... Wow! When I was a little girl, I took a great deal of comfort in thinking I had the strongest Daddy in the whole wide world! He was that and also more.

What memories linger in your heart and mind that help define both you AND your absent loved one?

Through the pain of death or loss, we miss the presence of what and whom we knew and experienced, while simultaneously grieving the self that interacted with that person or circumstance. We lament the loss itself, and also fear the change this brings into our existence.

At the same time, we recognize that the 'other' lived a life separate and complete outside our own realm. Do we mourn that too? I interacted with a Daddy who was gregarious and strong, but he engaged in a life filled with experiences that led to that overwhelming personality and strength. There is a difference, right?

Maybe I am asking the wrong question.

There is something in this thought about how we meet each other on this plane of existence; how we commit to one another and what that means. I want to explore this further. I inhabit this idea of my Path, which runs parallel to the paths of others and also intersects those paths. What exactly are those ties that bind us, and do they disappear simply because a loved one leaves or something I deem important ceases? Does it have to be over?

Maybe Grief is a way to acknowledge the combined separateness and togetherness of the relationship once shared. Death is a harsh slap that refuses to be ignored. *The End* seems so final.

Markers along Life's Journey can teach us this same process, as markers—or significant, even traumatic events—remind us that another person is not only the other part of the 'us' in the relationship, but also a True Self.

Borders are demarcations that signify one thing from another, or the difference between you and me; the difference between my Dad and me; the difference between me-in-the-present and me-in-the-past; the difference between you-in-the-present and you-in-the-past, the difference between now and then. Borders are formed the same way we form a Path: by our thoughts, beliefs, feelings, actions, imagination, connections, and reflections.

These borders become self-boundaries when they mark the edges within which the Self is contained. They highlight who and what I am, and this includes the capacity to acknowledge these border markers becoming boundaries of the self. My boundaries contain—among many other things—my thoughts, feelings, and beliefs about my Dad in tandem with my thoughts, feelings, and beliefs about death. My boundaries [of my self] also incorporate my imaginings even as these boundaries are shaped and changed by my actions. My reflections regarding this also determine where and how these self-boundaries form due to the way I process my memories, and dictate how I respond to this aspect of my Life's Journey. The same is true for you.

Interestingly, the way we Journey delineates borders, which then create boundaries that emphasize our True Nature and separate us from others. At the same time, these boundaries are shared borders with others close to us.

Lightbulb moment: My life's journey also had an impact on my Father's Path.

I laugh when I think of my healthy, handsome Dad who hung up the phone with an abrupt <click> the day he called to wish me love and happiness on my 40th birthday, and it suddenly occurred to him that time was passing . . .

"So how old are you today, Honey?" he asked me.
"I'm 40, Dad," I replied.
Silence.
"Then how old am I?" he asked.
I told him.
Click.
Dial tone. . . . . .

His initial bout with cancer was so easy that we probably did not realize how dearly *Fortunata* had smiled upon us. We talked about how blessed we were to live in a day and age with the miracle of modern medicine, blah blah blah . . . and we all went back to Life (whatever that is)!

And then . . .
        and then . . .

WAM!

This Thanksgiving he went into the hospital with all the alarm bells ringing, and now here we are again, but this time it is quite serious.

Now the real questions begin.

How do I deal with the end times of my father, knowing that this is a typical part of life? Have you asked yourself this question? Have you wondered (like me) how something that is supposedly 'normal' can feel so unreal? I have been on the other side of this with friends whose parents are aging: the hugs and handholding, the reassurances and affirmations. I know that people I love and admire have walked this path before, of course. That means it is do-able. Why then, does it feel so impossible?

Is feeling even the correct word?
I seem impervious to feelings, as if I cannot allow emotion to hold sway.
Feelings will influence my Path, and surely, properly understanding my feelings will help determine the direction of my Path.
Am I right?
But what if I simply do not know what my feelings are or where they exist?
What if I have trouble even locating my True Self?

Now it is my turn to be a daughter with a Daddy who is finally, old. Strange to think the words "old" and "Dad" in the same thought strand. He has lost 20 pounds on a frame that was already light. He is weak, and at times his mind wanders. He cried for the first time, ever, in my hearing. At these signs of my father's helplessness, my heart feels empty and cavernous even, and I wonder sometimes where to place new and sensitive feelings. I am learning to know a different version of my Dad.

- Dads change.
- They grow old.

How much of who we are originates and then is set in place from the very beginning of life?
Is that what "the ties that bind" means?
Is **who** I am linked to those who surround me?
Is **what** I am tied to those who share or parallel my borders?
Will that part of me (the shared border) disappear when my loved one leaves?

How much of my True Self is changed or even lost when I lose someone close to me and my heart?
How much of me is a reflection of those I love?

Do I voice these thoughts and feelings out loud?

Can they be articulated in a way that others will understand?

I have a good friend whose father joined Facebook about a year ago, and I friended him. His long status updates read like what someone would say in conversation as he walks out to fetch the mail, or what we might say in exchange to a neighbor over the garden fence.

I cannot imagine my father adjusting to Facebook. In fact, I tried to explain it to him once, and gave up. E-mail is probably going to be the extent of his reach. My friend's father, however, is a delight, and I admire his ability to carry-over his sense of a former time into the new media tools of the present. His Facebook posts remind me of my childhood and of a different time: of neighbors and a neighborhood when and where children and adults lived according to scripted roles assigned by society, and it all seemed to simple. Is that because I was young and naïve, or were we all?

I think of summer nights and playing kick-the-can with the neighborhood kids gathered right up to the moment of suppertime when the dads came home from work and the moms called us from the porch. We hopped on our stingray bicycles and raced home until the next day. I think of winter days and paper dolls, or playing games indoors with friends where the negotiations for the rules of each game would sometimes take longer than the actual games! We learned so much about each other, and ourselves.

-and I cannot imagine it any other way-

I would not trade any of that for modern video games, and I have to admit I do not understand the appeal. On the other hand, I cannot say that my generation learned how to get along with each other OR "the other" through all that play or negotiation time either. Perhaps there is no *right* way to play or make friends.

Do we learn to play from our very first moments and presence (or lack thereof) of our parents, or is it something else? Do we grow and shape ourselves according to those whom we love? Does each new relationship change the parameters of our existence, or is that too simple? It has something to do with the ties that bind, and this, of course is what makes death so hard. How do we untie those bindings, and do we have to? We spend a lifetime tying ourselves together, after all.

I was struck by a comment in a New Media Seminar I attended this year from a participant who said that she looks at status updates [on Facebook] from friends, and then she only talks [in person] to those who are not listed. Hmmmm . . .

I wonder how many people use Facebook as a distancing mechanism? I have thought about social media a lot this week. How public is something like the terminal sickness of a loved one? What about any tragedy or deep sorrow?

How do we ascertain or understand our presence through online status, and how do I announce a thing so private, yet also so important, knowing that others actually DO care and want to know? (I know that I want to know these things about my friends and loved ones.)

At a time like this, however, I find myself hiding from the superficiality. Maybe, I just exist in a private sphere at the moment, and social networking tools seem to exist for a more public use? Perhaps the efficiency of it just seems suspect.

Since I hurt, and the pain is so intense, maybe I distrust easy methods of communicating? In real time, I want the physical comfort of hands-on presence, and the people who actually know me and knew my Daddy.

> Who should I include in my Grieving Process?
> Is there a right way to do this?
> Do I –should I–include my siblings in my mourning?
> What about close friends?
> What is their role?

Have you thought about these things too?

Sometimes there are too many questions!

I want to reminisce and sometimes rant and rave!

"How lucky I am to have something that makes saying good-bye so hard."

~Winnie the Pooh[4]

Chapter 3: Saying Good-Bye

Increasing numbers of my father's friends email and post online, asking about him. Some are strangers to me, and some echo in the corridors of my memory banks. Their words ring of genuine concern and longtime friendship. Apparently they have not heard from him for a while, and they wonder:

- How is he doing?
- What is the prognosis?
- How does he feel?

Every time this occurs, I ask myself the same questions: I know what the doctors tell me, but

- How are you Dad, really?
- What does it fell like to be in this state of un-health?
- In the hospital for oh-so-long, and oh, while I'm asking;
- What does it feel like to be you?

Please Dad, I just want to know!

Yes, I have watched various friends and acquaintances say good-bye to a loved one, and now it is my turn. There is no way to prepare for this, and I think that saying good-bye is as unique as the individuals involved. It seems to be part of growing up. I am learning about myself as I learn about my father.

In what ways is this happening to you, and with whom? What I ask is, who has the biggest impact on your ongoing Journey now—who or what causes the questions that run through your mind?

I ask about myself even as I ask questions about my father. (This goes back to those shared borders.) Who is he/was he? I do not know this man whose friends have plastered his hospital room with cards and bouquets.

Surely it is common for adult children of divorced parents to attempt to piece together a story of a family that was not; to decipher what it says about personal identity. My father left home when I was 12 years old, and we were a barely functioning family for the years leading up to the end of my parent's marriage. After that I saw him only occasionally.

How would I know who he is? In the process of learning to say good-bye to my father, it seems I am learning about the man. I feel like I am saying "Hello!" Sometimes it is difficult to reconcile the man I am meeting now with the Daddy of my childhood.

This is typical in times of bereavement: we are faced with understanding—even reconciling the reality of a person we know/knew. Time, distance, other people, and just the relevance of separate lives means there are gaps in what we actually know. I stand in the present awash in memories wondering how much that stream makes me who I am today, yet also wondering how much of it is pertinent. Grief is complicated. Gaps and all.

When I was a little girl, my Dad was full of silly songs like the *Johnny Rebeck Song*[5] or the many verses of *So Long, It's Been Good to Know You,*[6] or this little ditty which was one of his favorites:

> *What a pwetty little bird the fwog are.*
> *When him walks him hops.*
> *When him don't hop*
> *Him sits on hims pwetty little tail*
> *Which him ain't got at all*
> *. . .almost hardly.*

These memories are wrapped up in giggles and delight.

If I close my eyes and imagine a perfect space, I think of walking along the bluffs overlooking the Bay. We called it Back Bay. I wonder, was that its real name? My Dad could skip rocks with ease, and I knew that it was important to count as the rock skimmed across the water landing on the shore across from where we stood.

He was always at home outdoors, and I can hear the hushed tone of his voice when he answered my questions.

He taught me how to catch dragonflies, and then let

them go . . .

When I was 10 years old my Dad took me trout fishing while camping at Navajo Lake in Southern Utah. I caught a golden trout, and at first I was so excited! The trout was large and gleamed in the sunlight, resting in my palm like a prize. I did not know that fish could cry, though, and when the trout started wailing, my heart wrenched in two. I looked up into my father's face, and he told me to RUN! Run back to the lake, and I did, as fast as my legs could churn and my feet could fly. I tossed that golden fish ahead of me, and I fancied it had a thought or two along with a wink for me as it swam away. My Dad told me a whimsical story about a grandfather fish who had eluded capture for many years, until a girl named Piper came along . . .

What I really remember about that day is walking along the lake and him looking at me with his head cocked to one side, smiling, and telling me that someday I would be a beautiful woman. His comment gave me untold confidence for many years! It was also part of those ties that bind. . .

On "Meet Your Father" day while I was in Junior High School, he came to talk not about his art, but rather about his passion for rock climbing. He was so dashing, decked out in his harness, with pylons, chisels, and carabiners in his tool belt, and a multi-colored rope with a grappling hook attached wound round one shoulder. My friends listened enthusiastically, and my teachers were enthralled. Yes, I was used to that reaction.

But that was just a glimpse. Time passed, and the father of my memories who was simultaneously and afterwards friend and lover of people I never knew, acted out his story in ways I could not have imagined. I do not know if I will get to know this person in the way he thinks of himself.

Does that matter?

Now he lies in a narrow hospital bed in a sterile room with a team of doctors and nurses as his everyday companions. He cannot eat due to a secondary infection, which does not have much to do with the cancer (which continues to spread), so much of his battle is tied up with the hospital-ness of being hooked up to tubes. The man of mirth who is my father is too solitary. He has too much time alone, which means he broods.

He enjoys hearing from his friends, even second-hand. It lifts his spirits, and he forgets his pain for a while. When I tell him who has contacted me, he responds with a story. That's the Dad I know . . . but it is only one facet of a complex man.

And aren't we all? Complex, I mean.

My father says he regrets missing out on so much of my life. I regret it too. I do not think he is going to get to know me in the short time we have left, but what is time: a human construct that describes the way we move through space, is it not? Will I learn more of who and what he is in ways that make sense?

Does that matter?

> But Dad, even so, where and how do I locate you?
> Are you in my heart now?
> Or are you in my mind?
> Both?
> What DOES matter?

Maybe it's all part of Saying Good-bye.

"That was the hard thing about grief, and the grieving. They spoke another language, and the words we knew always fell short of what we wanted them to say."

~Sarah Dessen[7]

Chapter 4: I Can Hear the Mermaids Singing. . .

I sit in conference with three doctors and a social worker, calmly discussing my father's "case." My eyes bore into theirs as if understanding can be found better in their intent than in the words they speak. The hospice doctor never varies from his script, even when I interrupt with my particular queries. When his sloooow response fails to address my question —or re-directs my focus—one of the other doctors jumps in to provide the necessary information.

Thank you, Dr. Hodap, for the fast-forward and for understanding that not all patients are the same, nor are their daughters. Thank you for taking us past the slow motion: let's-figuratively-hold-her-hand-and-pretend-we-don't-all-know-why-we're-here-so-we're-speaking-in-euphemisms-in-order-not-to-risk-hysterics-from-what-we-assume-is-a-delicate-daughter.

I have been a daughter to THIS father all my life, thus I have learned that life is about looking outward and for more. Thank you Daddy for teaching me the Adventuremental Life.

Back to the doctors . . . I listen and try to guess at my lines, so that I will be sure to say what is appropriate and at the proper moment. Presumably I mouth all the right words, yet hot, unbidden tears stream down my face, because this is my Daddy we are talking about, and he is lying just down the hall. Gone is the Daddy in my mind and I am confused. My Dad is virile and oh-so-alive!

Do they not know that about him?

I leave the doctors and walk down the hall to my father's sterile room. Outfitted in layers of antiseptic gown and thick blue rubber gloves. I lean over his bed.

How should I begin . . .and how should I presume?[8]

When I walk into his hospital room I do not want to recognize him. A voice echoes in my head:

> *That's not my father!*
> *The patient is etherized, lying on a table*
> *[approximating a bed],*
> *Let us go, Let us GO!*[9]

Who put that shrunken man who is mostly bones into my father's bed? It is he of course, but how can it be?

I am scared to touch him. I feel his arms, and I worry that I will ruin them; crush them maybe. His skin is paper thin and no longer pliant. He opens his eyes and knows me instantly. *He* smiles. He says, "I love you." He repeats my name. I whisper something funny up close near his ear, and he looks right at me with his fading blue eyes. I look deep into his and I laugh out LOUD. I call him Doggy Daddy. He laughs back, although it sounds like wheezing.

I clumsily climb into the contraption that is his hospital bed, and scoot next to him as well as I can, given all the layers and paraphernalia I am required to wear. I lay my head on his pillow. He nods and smiles, and I tell him a story about cutting through the water with the wind in his face. There is no time in his life that has not involved sailing and the swell of the ocean.

I talk about

- standing tall in the spray at the bow;
- the crack vs. the snap of the sails;
- the cry of the gulls;
- the silence of the morning sea.

I know the sea calls to him and always has. I whisper about the wisdom won from pain,[10] recalling our shared adventures rowing in the bay, beyond the jetty sometimes, and around the peninsula. I know about the lonely struggle.

I ask him if he knew how incredible it was [for me as a young child] when he ordered French Toast at the Jolly Roger Inn, and we shared it down at the docks. How afterwards, when he let me play on the thick rope coils while he traded stories with the grizzled old men, that I only half played, but mostly listened.

When I quote Aeschylus, he smiles. I return to T. S. Eliot, and he nods and smiles some more. He tries to gesture with one hand because he knows, for we have been on an adventure or two.

"Yes," I whisper in his ear, and he knows me.
"Yes!" he croaks, and I give him a sip of water.

I tell him that I love him. He fastens his pale blue eyes on mine, those eyes so used to gazing out to sea. I do not wonder if I dare. I always dare. Will my kisses make up for kisses lost to all those years? I kiss his forehead and notice his thinning hair as I brush it off his forehead. He closes his eyes and I bend down to his ear to tell him I know he loved me and I also know he loves me now. His eyes fly back open, wider.

> *Did I dare say that?*
> *Disturb the Universe?*
> *In a minute there is time*
> *For decisions and revisions which a minute will reverse.*[11]

I am standing now. Will all the *I-love-yous* make up for words we never said? His lips move and I bend down to my father's face.

"I love you" he says in a raspy, hushed tone. The effort causes him great difficulty. Maybe it was always this hard. Maybe that explains it all. I stay close, and smile up against his face so he can feel it/breathe it, and he repeats, "I love you."

"I know it," I say. "I so love you." I say I understand, and refer back again to Eliot:

> . . . *and I shall tell you all.*

This is a game we play, and have since I was very young. He is fully awake now.

> . . .*I grow old . . . I grow old . . .*[12]

He smiles at the reference, and his eyes sparkle as his lips move in time with me as I recite the poem.

> *"We have lingered in the chambers of the sea*
> *By sea-girls wreathed with seaweed red and brown*
> *Till human voices wake us, and we drown."*[13]

He continues to nod and smile.

- I laugh and squeeze his hand with mine.
- His eyes tear and spill over.
- Tears stream silently down his cheeks.

He says my name again. He falls asleep and I mouth the words to the poem:

> . . . *but that is not it at all,*
> *That is not what I meant at all.*

Is it?

> *Who is that etherized man?*[14]

46

In my father's hospital room? [SEP]

I did not expect to be making decisions like these alone, about a man I hardly recognize … but that's just it—it is hard, and I can almost understand why people want to avoid the situation.

ALMOST

I want to turn my head to a trusted person next to me and ask

"What do you think?"

I want a sibling to chime in and ask the questions I have not yet thought of. I want a loved one to say those OTHER things—that I forgot— in a voice that is different from my own.

Instead, it is up to me to think of every contingency and be all those voices and people too. Have I sufficiently listened to my father during these past few months and noted his wishes, despite his unwillingness to talk about death and dying?

Despite his skill at dodge and parry?

Last week, when he told me we would go pick blueberries this summer, this was a particular reference to the cherished story from childhood: *Blueberries for Sal.*[15]

Robert McCloskey's books are more than fabulous stories. Not only did they depict childhood in Maine, but in OUR family they were very personal, as with all great books, written especially about me (and later also about my sister Deirdre too).

It was not Sal who went picking blueberries and could never seem to fill her little pail (because she ate them faster than she picked and saved them), it was me!

And when she was surprised by a bear–oh MY!! Of course, she was not afraid, it was all part of the adventure! Is this how we learn or adopt our attributes and characteristics?

Thank you Daddy for teaching me

to approach my fears

face forward, asking questions.

What questions should I ask now? I reject inevitability. I deny "meant-to-be" as if those three words can quell my sorrow. There is no overarching reason for my Dad to die, any more than I can find a reason for him to have left our family home so long ago.

- Before I was done being a kid.
- Before I knew what it meant to have a Dad.
- Before I could say good-bye.

How can I know how to feel or what to do in this situation? I barely knew this man, and yet, he is my father. That means something so profound, it tugs my heartstrings. Dad, three weeks ago, you told me you wanted five more years. You asked me if I would give you another chance; if maybe you could learn to know your grandchildren. You said they deserved better, and you told me stories about your grandfather, whom you loved and admired.

Of course, Doggy Daddy.
If you are there, I will be too.
I will pick blueberries, and I will walk along the cliff
side of my great-grandfather's property, with various
remnants from the Revolutionary War in the
backyard.
We can look out to the sea together, you and I.
You asked for five years, and then you paused and
said, "How about just one summer more?"

Dad expressed more than a desire for blueberries; he wanted all of it.

> How do we accept the end of an adventuremental life? How does an Adventurer just stop?
> How about ANY life that can be described that has been shared and experienced?

> How do we know what questions to ask and who knows how to answer them?

The doctor says they have a term for that: negotiating with death. He says this gently as if he imparts new information. **Ha!**

His words make me laugh inside as I imagine the grim reaper vs. grim reality, and I wonder at the difference? Either way, no denial is possible, and both are inevitable. I reach deep within and face my contradictory feelings.

- Is there any peace to be found?
- . . . a place inside that will help me laugh and also love?
- . . . and also love myself?

Now you lie there sleeping, Dad, and the doctors tell me you only mumble incoherently. But you woke up and talked to me today! I no longer fear to touch and hold you. I think I know you after all. You will not break from something so mundane as a daughter's touch.

But that ol' balrog called Cancer?

That's a different story . . .

So, what happened to that outlandish man I ~~know~~ knew? Dad, I was thinking recently how you used to insist we keep the house at ridiculously cold temperatures in the winter, lecturing to us about something called "The Great Depression."

What do little kids know about these things? We shivered while we dressed for school, sitting on top of the floor heaters.

We never guessed that it had something to do with saving money or "thriftiness" because that was <u>never</u> your style. We thought —maybe— it was part of your dramatic flair, and we were playing a part in the drama. Why would we EVER think it had anything to do with a budget?

In that same time period, you came home with a glitter-gold dune buggy with a white leather top. Oh, it was crazy fancy, and the adventuremental times associated with that car were plenty! Do you remember sitting in one of those perennial traffic jams of southern California with rain POURING down, and in and through all the myriad cracks of the leather top, with the radio playing *It Never Rains in Southern California*, which you cranked up full blast while you laughed your uproarious laugh. We all sang along, dripping wet. YES! Do you remember, Dad, do you?

Are you deep inside recalling those times? You were part of my earliest adventures and discoveries. How can the adventuremental life just end? And now I am sad because I will never be able to tell you about

the mermaids I heard singing . . . and even found.

I miss you before you are gone, and well ... in so many ways you already are.

Sleep, now.

I hear you begin mumbling about your dreams, and before long, you disappear into thoughts that belong only to a dream world of your own. Of course I am more than certain you have heard the siren song yourself.

Today a hospice volunteer is playing folksongs for you with a banjo. You are sleeping, but I know somewhere, deep inside, you love listening to the jingles.

> And still. . . I do not need to travel long or far to find the YOU inside of ME.
> The shared Adventuremental Life can bridge our lives & worlds, and maybe time.

Shared Paths are shared borders are shared lives.

How much of your life is a shared path, which formed a shared border and a shared life not just with your loved one who has died, but with others, too?

Have you been able to gather and tell these stories to each other?

What did you share with your loved one who now is gone?

This process creates new borders and even shared boundaries of the Self.

This process allows Gratitude to form.

Thank you for an early world full of songs and tunes, and for giving me childhood friends like Stevenson, Homer, Eliot, Frost, and Keats, along with all the others.

- Thank you for these avenues to other interests and other people's lives, Dad.
- Thank you for the rich gift of poetry.
- Thank you for the mermaids.
- Thank you for living it;
- ... for leaping into the abyss.

"Tears soften the soul, clear the mind, and open the heart."

Chapter 5: 'Twas Brillig

I spent my first years in Eastport, Maine, and I have lovely images in my mind filled with tulips, my Gramma Bee's kitchen, her Siamese cat, Michael, and a vague sense of merriment.

In later years I would hear adults call me a "reserved child" and I don't think I was serious so much as one who spent time thinking. Listening to my father's friends, I get the feeling that he did so, too.

Later, growing up in southern California, it did not get chilly very often, but I remember a few cherished days when the fog would roll in, and my Dad would call me to come walk with him on a

Misty Moisty Morning
When foggy was the weather.[16]

I was always happy that my little legs could keep up with his long strides. He pointed out each bird, told me stories, and of course recited poems. Nonsense poems were our favorites. I think I could quote the *Jabberwocky* well before I went to school. I always had a red cape when I was young, which was its own sort of story, and I recall many a time, walking with my father in the fog, listening to his wonderful voice, with me, chiming in where appropriate.

Somehow the image of me in my red cape belongs directly to memories with him. It is an iconic image of myself because of the association. Do the iconized versions of the memories we hold onto with those we love and mourn make it easier to process our thoughts?

Are they memory markers, perhaps, that operate as boundary stones for the Path that delineates not just what it is to be Me, but how my Path was shaped by my Dad, and what was his impact? This could hold true for all the significant relationships and events in our lives.

I will hold on to this image of me in my red cape, as it helps me walk the *Path of Grief*, continuing to process the Gabrielle-who-misses-her-Dad. This makes me wonder why I no longer own a red cape, and maybe it would help if I did? Am I still that iconic girl in some way?

Do you hold images of your self with your departed loved one that help define the iconic self in your mind? How can you hang on to those images?

Life was a bit outrageous growing up in my household, but it was brillig, and on days like those I described above,

> *All mimsy were the borogoves,*
> *And the mome raths outgrabe.*[17]

A few days before he died, my father was lucid for over two hours. I sat next to his hospital bed holding his hand when suddenly; he opened his eyes, and said,

"There you are!"
I responded, "And you're here too!!"

He smiled his REAL smile and I knew my Daddy was
in the bed instead of that other guy who was just a pile
of bones wrapped in skin.

"We're both here," he said. "How nice."

I asked him if we had a quorum, and he looked at me
with the old twinkle in his eye and replied with a solemn
nod,

"I think so."

He grabbed my hands with both of his; using that
familiar strong potter's grip he had,

"Tell me a story, honey."

I asked him if he wanted me to read to him, and he said,

"No, tell me a story."

So I did. In the very same way he had, once upon a time
in a small town by the sea:

"*Once upon a time. . .*

. . . there was a man who had a little girl named
Piper. . ."

He wanted more than just a made-up tale, so I told him a true story about spelunking in the California desert where the cave was so dark, that even when we put our hands in front of our faces we could not see them. I followed him and his flashlight, but he was never the kind of father who coddled.

I held out my hand to guide myself by way of the closer-than-close walls, but I touched something furry/bristly. My mind imagined a monster spider, and I immediately withdrew all contact-- **YIKES!**

Since the Borrego Mountain earthquake of 1968 that flung me across the yard and dashed me to the ground as I unsuccessfully tried to run toward the anticipated safety of my father's arms even as he beckoned, ever after, my vivid imagination had no problem foreseeing the ground opening up and swallowing me at will. There, in that cavern, in the dark, I thought of the possibility of stepping into a hole, and similarly disappearing forever. Then I remembered the rope that linked us, and that my Dad remained in front of me:

"Daddy, are you there?"

He grunted.

Ok, so far, I was safe.

With a Dad like that, life was always an adventure, and I learned to fare forward, eyes open, even when I could not see. There are many things to be afraid of in life, but the scariest are those that cannot be predicted or named, am I right?

Maybe naming them in advance reduces the fear:

Beware the Jabberwock, my [daughter]!
The jaws that bite, the claws that catch!
Beware the Jubjub bird, and shun
The frumious Bandersnatch!

My Dad would cite these lines with me as if they were full of wisdom, and perhaps they were: Shun danger, but not by pretending it did not exist.

We often camped in the Santa Rosa Mountains. Once we found a wonderful spot that boasted a granite slab, fortuitously tilted to resemble a stage.

All it took was Dad's comment: "Well, look at that: a stage."

. . . and we were off! My brother, sister, and I produced marvelous productions, which evolved into fantastical dances wearing our blankets as capes or wings as we flitted and leapt about. Life is so magical in the woods.

Higher up the mountain, and long before we came along, someone built an enormous tree house with an even larger staircase to ascend into the massive redwood tree. I love tree houses, but those stairs!

They surely were carved by long ago giants because each step was so far apart that standing on one, the next was at waist height with the nothingness of air and the height and fear of falling in between each riser. Ohhhh, that was a long climb. About halfway up, when I was sure I felt the reality of gravity pulling me back, down toward earth, I complained to my father that this was not a do-able enterprise for a girl who was not yet 10 years old.

He stood there at the top, so tall against the sun and looked at me, thinking for a full minute or more. Then he asked me what I was going to do the next time something was not easy? "And the next?" "What if you had to do something in a hurry, will you hesitate like this?" he asked.

And, as in uffish thought he stood,
The Jabberwock, with eyes of flame,
Came whiffling through the tulgey wood,
And burbled as it came!

I distinctly remember thinking that the stairs and HE were equal foes. By which of them would I rather be defeated? And then I realized that conquering one meant beating both...oh Frabjous Day!

So, I climbed to the top.

My Dad nodded at me, turned, and we went inside the tree house.

Trees, mountains, caves, boats—my Dad was an explorer. Many who knew him can speak to that aspect of him. Now I am an explorer, too. I lead the Adventuremental life he taught me.

I am struck by this aspect of our relationship: the activities and tendencies that we share and enjoy without the need for being together. This is a sort of glue that not only calls attention to our border sharing, but also lets me know why this is so painful, now. There are so many aspects of my Self that now lack the part that was my Dad.

Over the years he would call me occasionally. He would express delight over my victories. Nothing seemed too small; everything was worth celebrating by way of song or verse.

And, has thou slain the Jabberwock?
Come to my arms, my beamish [girl]!
O frabjous day!
Callooh! Callay!'
He chortled in his joy.

Who doesn't want to be Beamish?

Approval from one's father … being noticed by my Daddy. Is that what Beamish means: the pat on the head, or is it rather participating in each other's Paths, Dad, so somehow I will learn to understand? Is this about how good it feels when paths intersect?

I say all this, yet *Frabjous* was a distant joy, because it was always a telephone conversation, and then you had to move on. Or perhaps that's what *Frabjous* means… just a few minutes– that's all you get– and then it is time to keep going. Maybe *Frabjous* is something else.

Maybe *Frabjous* means pay attention: to the steps under your feet, to the heights you have to leap, to the sounds near and far, and to the splendor of the trees. Maybe *Frabjous* is just about the smell and feel of beautiful green grass or dancing in the trees, and it has been there all along.

- Other places...
- Other people. . .
- Callooh! Callay!

Flit and leap on a stage made of tilted granite or any other plane of existence, and then

- . . . and then. . .
- move on.

Meanwhile, the world moved on too. . .

And the slithy toves did gyre and gimble in the wabe. . .

And then . . . I arrived one day in a hospital room, where my father was no longer a hero who could fight every foe and grimly laugh in the face of unpleasant reality.

On that AwfulWonderful day when my Daddy was lucid for over two hours and I got to be with him–really with him–we talked and smiled and it was real. And then he slipped away. I had to talk to the doctors anyway—I had kept them waiting—and then it was time to go back to his house and studio to keep sorting and managing the other parts of life.

- Reality.
- Existence.
- Imagining what is next.

Belonging

Of course I come *home* to Eastport and think about belonging.

I question hometown-ness and whether or not it is a made-up construct to justify a static existence, or if it bolsters identity. I wonder what or why I feel what I have felt that makes it so unique. It is difficult to describe what a coming-home like experience is in just a few short days. The town is quaint; I feel relaxed. Walking along the sidewalks gives me a sense of normalcy. Greeting the various people and visiting those who knew my Dad and knew me when I was young feels natural. Standing on the docks offers peace. I think it feels like HOME.

But what is that?

- Belonging
- Community
- Peace

Do you have a place where you can go? Can you travel to a home or a place of belonging that adds to your healing process just by being there?

I was not going to go back to my Dad's hospital room so soon, but I did. I am forever glad.

I suited up in all the anti-infectious gear: the gown, the gloves, the rigmarole, and I went to his bed. I leaned down and whispered a few words in his ear.

He said my name aloud, but he was asleep. I crawled into his hospital bed with him again as best I could with all the extra paraphernalia in the way, and then the flood started. I began to cry a little bit, and then more poured out. I could not stop it. How could I have known a gushing river would burst through the dam of appropriateness and strength I try to project and mix with the *I-Love-Yous* coming from my mouth and the giant tears I did not know were waiting behind my eyes? How do anyone's eyes stay in their head with such pressure swimming and bleeding onto a pillow?

I love you Daddy. I am going to miss you, I thought to myself.

"Good-bye" I choked on the liquid words.
"Good-bye honey," said my sleeping, dreaming Daddy.

After awhile, I stood outside my Father's hospital room, looking through the glass window, watching him sleeping and slipping away, thinking about leaving and what that meant, trying to understand I would not see him again. I had other people's stories in my mind now. I knew about his friends who were beginning to be my friends too.

I ruminated; I cogitated; my head reeled; the world roared in my ears.

I recognized why he had fought so hard and also wondered why he chose the battles he did. Some of his friends in other places wonder, still, why he went back to his hometown and also why he stayed. I do not. Death and dying can bring a sense of understanding, even though it hurts. The loyalty and sense of belonging he felt for that Down East place was fierce, and I understand it. Maybe it's all about finding and holding onto a piece or essence of the Self, however small or far away.

- A sense of place
- Locus
- Belonging
- Identity

In the end, something else happened. One can beware the Jabberwock, I suppose:

"The jaws that bite, the claws that catch."

One can even beware the jubjub bird; But the Frumious Bandersnatch? I think it got him, and that is also one of the risks in life. Apparently bladder cancer is a side effect for people who work with dyes, and my brilliant father was a MASTER not only of clay works but he mixed his own glazes. We all know that. We know about his famous book of glazes and how he mixed those potions like no other human being ever has or will. He understood his art. There is every chance that in the end, the Frumious Bandersnatch was the culprit.

He took his vorpal sword in hand: Long time the manxome foe he sought —So rested he by the Tumtum tree,
And stood awhile in thought.
One, two! One, two!
And through and through.
The vorpal blade went snicker-snack!

So he died.

But boy did he live!

"Give sorrow words; the grief that does not speak,
Whispers in the overwrought heart and bids it break."

~Shakespeare[18]

Chapter 6: Rituals & Formulas

During the dying months, I repeatedly traveled back and forth between Texas and Maine, and as I did I changed roles along with the suitcase/briefcase combination. Depending on my role, my entire demeanor would change. I lived on auto-pilot. Professor-self in Texas taught classes, met with students, showed up for committees, graded papers, and tried to hold the daughter-self at bay. The daughter part of me constantly distracted every other role by making plans to fly to Maine (fly to Portland, then rent a car and drive to the hospital or to Eastport), and be there in every way possible-- then come back and catch up with the work I had missed. The constant refrain: try not to let my work suffer or let slip the OTHER relationships and commitments that must be maintained: don't let anything drop along the wayside. In the meantime, I talked to my father's doctors almost daily: the doctors who kept me updated on my father's [lack of] progress. The connection was bad in my basement office, so I perched outside in the cold stairwell, straining to hear Dr. Hodap's cellular voice, and tried not to yell my questions in order to be heard, yet desiring privacy.

Inconceivably, time went by, while the mundane everydayness of it fed my sense of no-time, and belied the serious implications we talked about.

The doctor's messages revolved around the need for my presence, and I weighed my love and obligation for my father against the necessities of my ongoing "real" life. How can that be a fair comparison?

What is real life?

My mind rebelled at this impossible juxtaposition. How could I choose? Of course I must go. To acknowledge the markers on the Path is part of living, and showing up for death is important, even when death takes its time.

> Have you been faced with these
> decisions?
> comparisons,
> evaluations of what is more important,
> or what is more pressing?
> During life-altering, life-shattering
> moments,
> How do we decide?
>
> What if we make the wrong choice?
> Is there a wrong choice?

Maybe what is important is acknowledging
the moment

    . . . and to show up.

Before he died, Dad refused to talk about death or
"after," and told me to "just take care of everything."
He said I would know what to do.

Oh my.

How could I know what it would be like? How could I
predict how difficult it would be to act decisively once
the gravitational pull of Grief grabbed hold when he
died?

I am going through his things

and I hate calling the abundance of the

evidence that was someone's life: "things"

and I think back to my father's rock climbing days as I
sort through his gear: the pylons, rope, and grappling
hook. If only I could use these tools to catch hold of a
proper path. If I could use a chisel to fasten myself in
just the right place, and take those carabiners to connect
the necessary elements to make everything fit together.
Maybe then, I would know what decisions to make as if
there were a checklist for me to follow.

Taking action comprises those things we do that move us forward in time to form our Path (or a portion of a Path). We act, interact, and react, even as we are in the process of thinking, feeling, believing, imagining, connecting with others and remembering.

We search for coping skills and instruments or tools to help. All of this activity is intertwined and continues to form the Path. These processes continually determine *where* the Path leads. I keep thinking: what if I don't know where I am going or even where I want to go? Have you felt this way too? Sometimes it manifests as a sense of rushing or a hurriedness.

Some of this is formulaic and even ritualistic. Comfort can be found in mundane tasks. Planning a funeral means:

- Flowers
- Reserving a location
- Putting together a program
- Making announcements—and doing these in appropriate ways.
- Have we forgotten anyone?
- Music and food
- Guest accommodations
- Paying the bills,
- Contacting the authorities,
- Paperwork with the government
- and lawyers.
- Paying taxes,
- and sorting through the decades of a loved one's life.

- Sorting
- Gifting
- Crying
- Marveling
- Reminiscing,
- and yes, more sorting and cleaning, because there is so much to be done.

All of it is part of the process.

- Accepting condolences,
- Writing thank you notes,
- Holding others who cry,
- Crying alone
- and crying with others,
- and continuing to sort.

This is all a part of the ritual of death.

Every type of human pain carries its own rituals and formulas, both public and private. There is paperwork;

- legal work;
- people who must be contacted in person
- and by mail;
- hands to be held;
- handkerchiefs to be soaked;
- bills to be paid;
- notices to be written;

. . . and mostly there are questions about what is next?

Somewhere or somewhen, someone will say something about life "going back to normal," and it will be the craziest thing that has ever been uttered in the history of the world, but people who pretend to be sane will treat it like a rational statement, and maybe. . .

. . . maybe, if we are not careful we will believe the lie. No, life has changed, and no one else gets to decide what or when is "normal."

When we travel the *Path of Grief*, we move at our very own pace and in our own way. This is a Truth. To be True to the Self, the *Path of Grief* cannot be charted by anyone else but the Self.

Follow the rituals and the formulas because they are time tested and part of human life. They will provide border markers that will help you establish a sense of reality and an ability to ground yourself. They do not, however, determine how you feel, nor do they describe your Journey. The rituals provide future memories about THIS time, and that, too, is part of the Journey.

I continue to travel back and forth between Texas and Maine; between selves. It is a balancing act that I am continually learning.

As I sort through my father's things, I find thousands of hand-written letters he saved, and I am happy that mine are among them. I am surprised and delighted to see the correspondence between him and my children, too.

I am so glad that he knew them and they knew him. I have wondered before what they thought of him since his physical appearances in our lives were so rare.

I think about the traditions or customs he started, which I have carried forward. I recall when I was young and we were on our way to any camping location; how he was prone to stop randomly, and get us out of the land rover to search for garnets among the pebbles along the side of the road, or to point out and identify the names of the foliage and undergrowth.

Sometimes we stopped to pick wild berries, search for red salamanders in a shallow stream, or catch horned toads. This is the adventuremental life, and I continued this practice with my children camping and hiking with verve.

I thought of him on a camping trip when I woke them one morning at dawn to catch the deer drinking at a pond close by. I imagined him with us when my kids and I took a midnight hike under a full moon in Yosemite National Forest under the looming shadow of El Capitan. I also thought of him as I read bedtime stories to them each night, and hoped to instill in them a love for literature.

My father influenced my children indirectly through the gift of wonderment he gave me, but he also gave them a glimpse up close when he visited occasionally. I distinctly remember the time he came to see us, and the boys were so excited to take him hiking and show him their outdoor skills.

Even little two-year old Amanda fell under his spell, and she walked the three-mile trail we took, and then promptly fell asleep at the summit!

I understood her need to keep up with his tireless spirit. I loved watching him show her how to attract and feed squirrels, as I recalled being in her shoes once upon a time. That was the year those fuzzy red-colored boulders abounded, and we discovered that they were red, because they were covered in multiple layers of lady bugs!

Parts of his legacy are these stories that are the shared memories that have been passed down as custom in our lives. Now his great-grandchildren go camping and hiking with their parents—my children and his grandchildren—and hear the stories, discover the names of places and wonderful natural spaces with garnets and salamanders to discover.

Is that a Formula for Life?
Is that part of the Path?
Thinking is not just about thinking about anything pertinent to the situation of the exact moment in which we find ourselves.

It is also to think and notice our self: thinking.
As we focus, we see that we are thinking, and thinking about thinking.
The thought process is powerful, and forms Paths of Paths.

All of it [shared Path] was part of the Path that brought you here, and you will take it forward, too.
Can you identify the specific pieces that have become custom and customary in your Journey?

We think and ask questions. We follow formulas and establish rituals and customs. We live the Adventuremental life and pass it on.

"To weep is to make less the depth of grief."

~Shakespeare[19]

Chapter 7: On Grief & Missing Pieces

I cry a lot these days. I am a pool of sadness, and I wonder at its depth. I sometimes imagine a bottomless pit that I will fall into in this despair I feel. Is there a limit to sorrow? I once climbed a glacier mountain: a nine-mile hike upwards with a perfect picnic spot before the final, last mile at a memorably beautiful flower field surrounding a glacier lake with no known bottom. The deep blue water was so penetratingly cold, that "cold" is an insufficient word. Maybe the loss of a loved one is like that.

My Dad is gone from my life and the place where he existed has been ripped out of me. There is no known bottom. Do you feel like that, too? Do you feel the loss, but also wonder if there is any end to the pain? Is that a possibility—to just spiral ever downward into the pit of despair? This seems like a bleak prospect; that I might feel like this with no end. The hole that was left behind the place he used to be –wherever and whatever that is/was feels bottomless, and there is nothing to fill it with but grief. At least that is what I feel, and feeling is all I have and am.

Maybe it is less a feeling, but an imagined state of being as I look towards a future life of sorrow: my self, filled with tears.

I did not ask for this; so how can it be so much a part of my being? Rationally, I know death is a normal part of life, but I do not seem to be in control of my so-called rational processes.

I was/am so unwilling for this event to occur. No one asked Me: "Excuse me, Ma'am, is it ok if we take away your father forever?!"

People ask me how I am, and I say "ok," meaning "as well as can be expected," but do they know about the bottomless pool of sorrow? The anchor that drags me downward?

The Nothingness.

Maybe it is like a piece missing from the center of a puzzle that becomes forever unrecoverable. Try as one might, a hole remains in the picture, and to insist there is not a hole requires that we change the nature or boundaries of the original configuration.

All of this is a:
- Puzzle
- Configuration
- Conundrum
- Enigma
- Challenge

What once was is no more: daughter-ness. How much of my daughter-self depends upon my Dad's corporeal existence?

Has your *Path of Grief* changed you too? Do you feel changed? Can you name it?

People proffer platitudes and pleasantries meant to placate. Pain is part of this process, though, and their words fail to penetrate. It is not their fault; they are sincere, yet so am I. Do I need to pretend to be "ok" to make these people feel better? It seems like it.

Plain and simple: the sadness is as inescapable as the fog I see outside the window in the morning hours. East coast fog is not like Carl Sandburg's little cat feet.[20] This fog is more like a blanket or a shroud. It overlays everything and covers up the missing parts. I cannot connect the puzzle pieces and make a whole.

Like Life and Death

- I miss you Daddy.
- I miss your jocularity and your intractability.
- I miss your laugh and your growl.
- I miss your code of honor that I search for in every man I meet,
- and I miss your sense of adventure.
- I miss your stories and your ability to "go there."
- I miss the twinkle in your eye,
- and I miss your piercing glare when you were about to explode at some inanity in the world—or closer by.

- I miss your little ditties, your clever stories, and our deep discussions and analyses of political ramifications rambling the globe through time and space.
- I miss all those missing years when you went to find yourself and forgot to perch in one place long enough to grab hold.
- Why did you do that, yet how could you not?
- You are / were larger than life.

You always called me Darling Daughter, and just last night I was going to call you on the phone to verify a story that someone here in town told me, and then of course, I stopped short—because you are not on the other end of the phone, are you?

Once you told me about a man who was so mean, he shot Santa Claus. Now, in the present, I have the sleigh bells [you gave me] from the horse of that Santa-shooting-man, and you are not here to tell me the missing piece of the story. Missing pieces equal more heartache, because I miss that part of myself.

I feel lost.

I look out the window at the shroud of fog that is the sky, and see the ground covered in moisture. Something must be wrong, because I feel so dried out.

- *I cried myself out yesterday.*
- *And the day before.*
- *And the day before that.*

Perhaps there is no such thing as a bottomless pool of grief. Maybe grief is a desert.

Once, when I was nine years old, we went camping in Death Valley. Dad was on a quest to develop a glaze that had a lichen-like quality. He was also interested in the deep colors of the desert found only in the crevices of certain stones: burnt, yellow ochre; deep, red umber; and variegated turquoise. Camping was a normal, often thing for us, for adventures are found anywhere one goes, but most especially in the lonely places.

We went to Death Valley with our friends, the Somersons, and Patrice was just my age. Patty and I wanted to go exploring, and we called out our plans to my Dad from the rise of a dune. He waved his arm in reply and answered something about having left his hip pack of chisels over that dune, so would we please pick them up on our way back?

We thought we knew what he said. Unfortunately, the tricks of the wind sprites of the desert fooled both us AND him, and neither of us heard what the other truly said. Patty and I took off, enjoying each other and the desert in the way that little girls can, while looking for the chisel pack. No sign. We thought, maybe he meant the next dune, maybe the next one, or the next. . . .

We were collecting little stones and talking, and eventually our canteens went dry. We decided we better go back to camp and report our inability to find the chisels. When we returned, camp was empty!

(We found out later that what my Dad really said to us was to keep walking over the dune, because they were going to relocate the camp.) Who knew?

Back at camp, we found retreating tire tracks of the dune buggy and land rover from our family and the jeep from Patty's, but the wind had already wiped most of the trail away.

We called with our loudest, strongest voices, only for the gusts of the wind to be thrown right back at us. We climbed the nearest dune and looked around. No sign of any cars or people.

What should we do?

We yelled at the top of our lungs, and then listened intently. Nothing. We slid down the dune and climbed the next. We yelled again, and listened. Again, nothing. We tried to think logically, and pinpoint our likely location, but really all we did was become hopelessly lost since every dune looked like every other dune. We tried again and again, and continuously yelled for our fathers. The sun was hot, and we were parched.

Our lips were chapped and the mirage effect made everything hazy. We set up a pattern, and climbed to the top of each dune, yelled, and then waited to hear nothing.

Eventually, our voices became croaky whispers. The sun grew hotter, and it was well past midday. We had no water.

We were lost in Death Valley.

We decided to simply choose the very tallest dune, climb it, and wait for our Dads to find us. The winds were strong and the sand stung our skin. The sun was blistering. We also knew that nighttime would bring worse dangers.

Every once in awhile we would pretend to yell "Daaaaaddyyyy!!!!!" but it was really just pantomime because our voices had been sandblasted away hours before, and we had no sense of distance or direction left.

Even if we had a sound to make, our words would have been instantly carried away by the sandy wind whips that flailed and snapped at us, huddled on top of the dune.

Hours later, we heard a gunshot! We looked in the direction of the sound, and several dunes away was my Daddy, standing on top of that sand mountain with his arm raised and a gun in his hand shooting into the sky, hoping we would hear it. We did.

Apparently it was not the first shot, but it was the first one we heard. We stood up and tried to dance and yell. He came running and sliding down his dune, up and over, and rushed to encompass Patty and me in his giant arms, with tears and laughter mixed together:

"I thought I lost you," he cried, smothering his voice into my neck, kissing my cheeks, my ear, my forehead, and looking at my incredibly burnt, chapped face.

"I knew you would find us" I tried to say, clutching him as tightly as possible.

I don't remember the walk back to camp. I think he carried me, because I vaguely remember Patty's Dad appearing, swooping her up, and taking her quietly down the dune. I wanted to apologize about not finding the chisels and I remember my Dad hushing me; telling me to sip water from his canteen; not to worry; to rest my voice.

And now I am lost *in* this desert of grief so full of aloneness, and there is no Daddy to find me, no matter how long I yell, or wait, or wish. I have no map to show me a way through this endless array of sameness: sand-sucking dunes to climb again and again.

I think I reach some kind of pinnacle, and then look around to see only more of the same. I am parched. I am worn out. I have no energy left for regular life, because all I see ahead is the struggle with no way out.

I have to find my own way, and because others have done it, it must be possible. But it is difficult to understand that. I feel stiff and lifeless. Like my chapped lips that cracked and bled after my long day in Death Valley, I sometimes feel chapped and unable to move lest I break. I wonder if I react to others the way that I should?

The fog is thick in my mind, and I do not know what I will be like in My Imagined Future without that missing piece that was my Daddy. I do not know where the highest dune is, and I do not know if that is the answer.

Have you felt immobile in this same way: chapped and dry on the outside, yet broken and tearful on the inside?

Feelings are powerful,
and can even be contradictory.
How do we explain them?
I don't think we have to explain them,
but it helps to describe them.

Feelings are utterly valid.
Feelings just are.
Feelings need to be felt.
Sometimes, the lack of feeling—the desert—is the worst kind of feeling, because of the brokenness.
It's good to know that this is normal, and part of the *Path of Grief*.

Lists are helpful. Sorting through my Dad's paperwork, I come across a list, scribbled in his hand:

- Catacombs
- Labyrinths
- Subtracts
- Gates
- Doors
- Particles
- Windows
- Fenestration
- Hinge

What were you thinking about, Dad?

- Going in or coming out?
- Openings or Closings,
- Passages or just the process?

The practice is familiar to me, as I do this very same thing. I can almost jump in like *Alice through the Looking Glass*, and I want to. I wonder about your trail, and I listen for your footsteps and your voice Dad, the voice that no longer resonates in this world. It might not be present, yet I continue to hear it.

Where were you going with these words? It seems like you left yourself open to possibility . . .

Just last month you told me we would pick blueberries this summer, so I will do it for the both of us.

Even with the fog and the desert.

When the heart is cut or cracked or broken
Do not clutch it.
Let the wound lie open.
Let the wind from the good old sea
Blow in to bathe the wound with salt
And let it sting.
Let a stray dog lick it.
Let a bird fly in the hold and
Sing a simple song
Like a tiny bell and let it ring.
Let it go.
Let it out.
Let it all unravel.
Let it free and it can be
A path on which to travel.

~Michael Leunig[21]

Chapter 8: Ringing the Bell

Sometimes I feel abandoned or maybe a better word would be avoided. I do not mean abandoned by my father through his dying, but rather by people who otherwise surround me, but make themselves scarce in my *Path of Grief.*

- I get it.
- I understand.
- And yet —

85

I know that I tend to repeat the same words and phrases and I often tell the same stories. I understand they [the avoiders] do not have sufficient answers for me, but I feel like they should at least try.

I want them to know that if they slowed down just a bit and listened to me ramble, I might then find new and different words to say because the saying is so very difficult and I, too, am tired of hearing it. Still, it must be said. And said again. The Path is like that: road blocks require repetition and emphasis.

When I notice people avoiding me, or the well-meaning yet misguided souls who say things like, "Don't you think it's time to move on?" or "You know it's all for the best, my Dear" I cringe and despair a bit more. How about those who tell me "Everything happens for a reason," as if they know what I am thinking about/crying about at that particular moment!? As if my experience—or any human being's real life experience—can be summed up with a pithy saying, placed in a neat little package of a few short words that actually mean:

"Get over it!"

Get over what, exactly? How does anyone "get over" the living of life? There is no such thing as playing leap frog on the Path. Eventually, every step must be taken. No two people will travel in the same way or at the same pace, but this means exactly that: no one else can tell you how to pace the *Path of Grief.*

Is it possible to avoid the avoiders?

Or is that a case of "two wrongs don't make a right?"

Is there a way to simply smile and walk away?

Is it ok to NOT answer those who give wrong-minded,

ill-advised "advice"?

What do you think?

What works for you?

These thoughts remind me of an ancient fable my Gramma Bee told when I was very young, called *Belling the Cat* by Aesop:

> *It seems that a great council of mice gathered to discuss the terrible problem of the sneaky, voracious cat in their midst. Because of its sly maneuvers and its very sharp teeth, no mouse was safe.*
>
> *How could they track the dangerous feline? After much discussion, a young mouse came up with a fabulous idea: they would tie a bell on a string around the neck of the awful cat! The bell would ring as the cat slithered along mouse trails, thus warning the mice of their imminent doom. This seemed like such a great idea until each of the mice realized the problem: how would mice—or any mouse—put a bell on a cat?*[22]

No one wants to feel like the malignant cat in a world of little mice who would otherwise have a peaceful existence if not for the interruption of the cat's needs!

On the other hand . . . cats exist, right?

I want to think of bells in a different way. What if those of us who feel the need for comfort, could somehow ring a bell, and instead of running away, people came to listen, hold our hands, nod, smile, and cry with us? What would that be like?

What if ringing a bell was a signal that meant others knew to come and listen to the same stories and the same cries repeatedly? Would that be okay? I think the answer is yes, because the purpose is not to hear a story or gain new information. Rather, the purpose is to comfort and offer support on the *Path of Grief.*

Sometimes, listening is the greatest gift we can offer, but we might need a reminder: like a bell.

I am reminded of visiting Mont Saint-Michel off the coast of Normandy. This Benedictine abbey and the village that surrounds it were built in the eleventh through sixteenth centuries. The exquisite abbey is built on a crag, and can only be accessed according to the tidal cycles. The ascent is incredibly steep.

The castle abbey is built directly into the rock, so traversing it is the same as climbing a mountain. Because it is so large, the incline is not immediately apparent, but the length of time, and the repetition of climbing, winding, and climbing, up the stone stairs to continue to pass under the arch to reach the site, much less continue to the more beautiful levels weighs down the traveler.

It is a task to stop and enjoy the wonder and majesty of the experience and simply to fill the lungs for lack of sufficient air! Breathe, the adventurer tells herself, while looking upward at the continuing, winding, ever-rising stairs that remain.

The first time I visited the abbey I privately told myself that just reaching the top should come with some kind of reward, but I soon felt chastened, because I actually received something better than I could have imagined. Towards the upper level of the abbey is an open-air garden cloister surrounded by a quincunx colonnade. This leads to a magnificent gothic choir whose heights defy explanation. I arrived in time to view a young acolyte stride out to the middle of the stone floor and reach up with long arms to pull an extended, thick rope. The pull of the rope set forth the bells, which rang clearly over the mountaintop, calling us to prayer just as I slipped into a pew. Glorious sounds of Cistercian nuns filled the space. No description can adequately convey the beauty of that moment.

From this experience, this is what I imagine: that the beautiful sound of a bell is not meant to warn people to stay away due to danger or even annoyance. The sound of a bell is a welcoming sound meant to gather a community for good purpose. When we see someone in pain, we will respond as if to that bell, and go for the bell ringer's needs; not ours.

If we are the one who is ringing the bell (walking the *Path of Grief*) we have no need to apologize for the pain, the sorrow, the tears, the repeated stories, the need for comfort.

This is a centuries long tradition: people gather together and repeat songs, prayers, stories and mostly just sit together. A ringing, singing bell captures our awareness and adds significance to the markers on our Path. Bells mark so many moments. Ralph Waldo Emerson wrote:

> *I love thy music, mellow bell,*
> *I love thine iron chime,*
> *To life or death, to heaven or hell,*
> *Which calls the sons of Time.*
>
> *Thy voice upon the deep*
> *The home-bound sea-boy hails,*
> *It charms his cares to sleep,*
> *It cheers him as he sails.*
>
> *To house of God and heavenly joys*
> *Thy summons called our sires,*
> *And good men thought thy sacred voice*
> *Disarmed the thunder's fires.*
>
> *And soon thy music, sad death-bell,*
> *Shall lift its notes once more,*
> *And mix my requiem with the wind*
> *That sweeps my native shore.*[23]

Emerson's poem reminds us how bells often toll for death. They regularly remind us of its presence. This, too, is a very human part of life's Journey, as the tolling of the bell attests to the importance and value of life. In another way, the bell's echo affirms a pause in life, or closure for those who need it. Tolling bells accompany our dear one's Journey from this life.

Is it possible to think of bells in both ways: as the call to gather AND a way to accompany our loved one who is leaving?

Tolling Bells

I spent two years working for a Non-Profit Organization in South Korea, and took my three children with me. We lived in a local village and occasionally traveled around the country seeking historic sites and mountain retreats in the interior. One such visit taught me something about the personal meaning that travels alongside death throughout time.

One spring weekend we traveled to a Buddhist monastery built on top of a mountain. Arriving at the destination was quite an accomplishment partly because of the long hike, broken only by occasional rest stops at natural fountains of holy water.

The most striking feature of the temple monastery was a series of giant bronze bells as old as the eighth century, each weighing over 100,000 pounds.

Each bell is hung on its own column and has its individual ringtone and purpose. Many of the bells were originally cast as part of the funeral process, to guide the soul's journey to the next life.

I want to emphasize the specialization of the bells at the monastery we visited. One of the bells was hung specifically to call to those who were lost in the forests of the mountains. Another was hung on occasion to call those lost at sea.

The most memorable was a bell commissioned by King Seongdeok, best known as the Emile Bell. It is an especially beautiful bell that rang due to the death of an infant. The significant part of that bell is its ring tone which sounds like Emilee, the ancient Korean word for "Mommy."

- Memories
- Gathering
- Calling
- Ringing

What strikes me, even now, is how important these bells were (and are) for those who remain behind. We need ways to mourn. The centuries-old existence of these magnificent bells attests to this as a very human need. How do we find ways to express the grief beyond our words and tears? How can we ring a bell in a way that has meaning and is also useful? How can we remember to answer the call of the bell?

"Grieving is a journey that teaches us how to love in a new way now that our love is no longer with us. Consciously remembering those who have died is the key that opens the heart that allows us to love them in new ways."

~Tom Attig[24]

Chapter 9: Counterpoise & Equipoise

I heard someone say today: "I need to go home. My roots need water." I might not have paid particular attention a few months ago, but my ears perked up as we passed each other, and I thought about my recent journeys to my father's hometown:

- To my origins,
- to what has become a place of rediscovery,
- to a place of balance.

With Eastport literally surrounded by Atlantic sea water, I smiled instantly at the juxtaposition of roots and water, and now reflect on the strength and primal nature of the feeling tied to the tidal pull of the coastline. I feel it even here, in Central Texas as a yearning deep inside.

I guess my roots need water.

Where do you call home and is it the same thing as a hometown or family origins? What do you long for when you think of balance? How are these ideas related?

Lately I have pondered the extremes that exist on the *Path of Grief*—the feelings I have written about, for sure, and others, too. Sometimes I find myself thinking and acting in unaccustomed ways, or conversely, in the manner I acted before my father died.

This can make me feel uncomfortable, as if I am betraying the *Path of Grief* somehow, or dishonoring my father. Of course I tell myself this is ridiculous—there is no rule or obligation of eternal misery, but my feelings say otherwise. I want to find the balance that will allow me to get from here to there (whatever *there* is).

Could this be about touching base with my father's roots or even the place of his death? Is there a need to find acceptance of death via physical location? Perhaps it helps us understand the reality of the before-and-afterness of death. Maybe the *Path of Grief* is also about movement on a physical path, like visiting/re-visiting the place my father lived and died. In talking to others who have experienced the pain and loss that accompanies grief, I have found this running thread: the need to physically visit and reconnoiter the places and spaces our loved one spent the last period of life in order to continue the moving on movement that is Life, after.

I am certain I am not alone in processing the loss of someone I love while asking questions of myself and where I belong. I am not the first person to struggle with death or loss along with all the questions that parallel this path. I am also not unique in navigating the various feelings:

- Disappointment
- Discouragement
- Distraughtness
- Resignation
- Helplessness
- Hopelessness
- Misery
- Despair
- Grief
- Sorrow
- Anguish

Each of these exists on a spectrum, and each emotion feels different; each represents a different state of being.

How can we describe them to our self and to others?

The other part of this is not only do we not always feel exactly the same on the spectrum, but sometimes we do not feel ANY of these grief-related feelings. There are minutes and hours when anguish does not dominate, and as time goes by, those hours become an entire day and then several days, and even more.

Is that ok?

How do we find the balance between the highs and lows, or the semi-lows and super-lows, or whatever the range is in our emotions as we move along the Path?

This is like the idea of reflection via a light vs. a mirror. Holding aloft a light to better see the Path reveals a close-up view where I can learn more about the life of my loved one and even choose to follow it if I want. I can better see MY Path, and determine if it represents my emotional outlook and plans for life. The light becomes my focus on the Path and the mindfulness I pay to my Journey.

This is important: I do not want to focus purely on the emotions I feel while I am traveling on this *Path of Grief*, but rather focus on the Path itself, and acknowledge and recognize the feelings and emotions that occur as I journey. Once we get past the numbing every day existence of the Nothingness, and past the never-ending pit of sorrow, then it might feel like we are living on a roller coaster of emotions. Now it is time to focus on the Path itself, and accept the emotions as they come.

Shine a light on your Path: think about it and evaluate the location and the spaces and places you take yourself. Choose. You will know when it is time to move in some direction. It is okay to float along until it is time to move. YOU will know when it is time to choose to venture forth.

The Mirror of True Seeing

How will you know when the time is right? You will know through the other form of reflection: through the *Mirror of True Seeing*, which will become one of your greatest tools. Time out of mind, the Hero's Journey has included a crucial moment in the adventure [that is Life] when the hero must look into an important Mirror. The Mirror requires the hero to truly see, and remain looking.

In some stories it might seem like this is an impossible barrier, made only for the strongest of heroes, but this is not the case. The *Mirror of True Seeing* is first of all, about determining whether or not you are a hero, and that is something YouWonderfulYou know how to be. Answer: be yourself.

There is but one requirement to successfully looking into the *Mirror of True Seeing*: to see your True Self. Yes, it can be difficult. (In fact, there is probably something wrong if it is easy!) Looking into the *Mirror of True Seeing* is not a one-time thing, but rather becomes part of the Path that allows one to become a True, Authentic Self.

Looking into the Mirror offers a different kind of reflection than shining a light on the Path. The Light shows me the details of my personal Path. The Mirror shows me the details of my True Self. Used jointly, I can forge ahead, with confidence, ready to learn how to balance my life, even on the *Path of Grief* as it evolves.

I am sure I am not the only person to walk the *Path of Grief* paved with question upon question, focusing on what [who?] we have loved and lost, looking for traces of what once was and how that fits on my Path. Do I need to follow that thread? I am one of many who wonder about the pain of loss, if it is truly possible to carry the burden, and for how long? I am part of the human tradition of those who have discovered that balance is required to continue this Journey, because it is multi-faceted, and I have much to learn about MY Path, as do we all.

As I sorted through my father's books last month, how interesting it was to find so many shared titles, along with the *Tom Sawyer* edition with the Norman Rockwell illustrations that he gave me, then took back, which I then took back, which he then took back, which I then took back, which he then took back, which now I hold . . . permanently.

Oh, how I miss that game!

And Daddy, I didn't know you read so many of my favorite books . . . along with all the rest. Did you first give me Richard Bach? I see him on your shelves. Bach wrote:

You are not the child of the people you call mother and father, but their fellow-adventurer on a bright journey to understand the things that are.[25]

Dad, the history books on your shelves, and those many conversations we had —or should I say discussions, debates, and even arguments— did they and you contribute to my vocation as a scholar? Does my craving for the atmosphere of archives, the smell of musty tomes, and the feel of limestone walls have anything to do with this thirst for knowledge and understanding that you instilled inside me? Where do we derive our inclinations, tendencies, habits, and dreams? Is it the nurturing of our roots? I think my roots have many sources. I suppose my Journey is more than just a discovery process, a hunger for roots, or even a return home. I am looking for the pieces of my True Self.

I keep thinking back to all the winters when you would come and find me before dinnertime each night to say, "Come on, let's go for a walk."

It was chilly in that nice, California evening sort of way. I clearly remember your impatience as I grabbed my beloved little red cape because we needed to 'get on with it!' We had places to go and things to talk about, which in my memory's eye is a blend of fast walking, deep talking, and even deeper listening, passing by the little butterfly tree (empty at this time of year), with me, holding together my cape so you would not guess that it was not quite warm enough, and possibly end our dialogue.

You and your intensity asking and answering all at once, not just allowing, but encouraging and accepting me at the same time while we both tripped over puddles. My mind raced in that wonderful calm feeling like rocks skipping over water, enervated by the chase for what might be said... next, if we could just talk hard enough.

You felt it too, I know.

Life is a journey toward a seemingly elusive goal partly because the journeying is so very delicious and sweet, and partly because it seems like it will never end. There is movement towards a next. But now I seem to have come to an end, or is it part of an end? Let's not say, "end," because it truly is not. Instead, this is like any worthwhile Journey: there are twists and turns, obstacles and even barriers. I will navigate this as I go.

And now ... I am circling back to my origins along with facing the end of my father's Journey, and learning how to separate the two paths, which requires a balancing act of sorts.

I find myself in dialogue with the father I knew, simultaneously with the man I am getting to know through the eyes of others even though my father is no longer physically present, and it becomes a different kind of passage. I am learning how to share you in my memories, Dad, and that can be difficult. I am discovering that you shared your Journey with many people of different stripes and ways of living, and I do not fully know how to meld my idea of you with everyone else's.

This kind of journey fits with the idea of pilgrimage. I love contemplating *The Path*, and how in historical pilgrimage, folks gathered to make a statement about themselves individually and as a group, along with the open declaration they made by traveling to a place that exemplified an idea or a belief. They traveled along well-worn pathways towards significant —usually sacred— destinations in the company of both friends and strangers. The idea was one of common interest and a shared goal.

To be a pilgrim was essentially a declaration of a willingness to share the Path with others, not knowing the outcome, but hoping for a share in the dream. Most of all, to be a pilgrim once, was to always thereafter be —and to have been--a pilgrim.

- Journeyer
- Traveler
- Wanderer
- Rover
- Pioneer
- Trailblazer
- Pilgrim

Will I sound trite if I emphasize my point by saying that to be a pilgrim has never been as simple as arriving at a destination, but about the dialogical relationship discovered and entered into along the way?

When I first began meeting the pilgrims from my father's journey—those who came after my childhood—I went through an entire series of emotions. At first, I felt like he had hidden himself from me, forging relationships with people outside my frame of reference, and separate from anything I knew about. I almost resented the information others gave me about my Dad, because they knew something about him that was real, yet it was so different than my knowledge! It took me awhile to recognize that his Journey—even the part he shared with me—was HIS, so naturally it encompassed a wide variety of journeyers and fellow pilgrims.

Have you encountered these thoughts?

Now that he is gone, I have my memories with him, and I have more. After my initial astonishment at discovering the lives he lived with other people I never knew (or even guessed at), now I am simply following his trail.

Sometimes it is rocky, with rubble underfoot as I am uncertain of the way ahead. The twists and turns have been unexpected! But it is indeed a joy to meet the people who knew him and want me to know the Don they knew. How great is that: the community that surrounded him that is reaching out to embrace me, his daughter? Enlarging my knowledge and understanding of him whom I loved so well, enriches the love I hold for him now. It also seems to expand backwards, along the Path of Memories to encompass the Time when he was part of my life, too. The better I know him, the more gratitude I feel for the Parallel Path and the many intersections with others' Paths, as well means the better able I am to balance the unfolding Path.

One of my Dad's sculptures displays this idea so well. He carved and assembled wooden beams into a life-sized sculpture he named *Equipoise and Counterpoise*. The various pieces of planed, carved wood reach out in diverging directions all starting from a single starting point.

The complex movement of the structure —*counterpoise*— somehow adds up to a sculpture that rests securely in balance, each piece holding its place securely in the whole —*equipoise*. This piece of art represents a series of adjustments that distribute the weight of the journey, or the need for balance in the stress and tension of the time and place. Maybe the many different aspects are part of what creates the balance of the whole?

- Struggle
- Reaching Out
- Being Human
- Building Community
- Movement

This is the way we choose companions, form friendships, and build community, and I do not believe it is a simple process. Much of it has to with occasion, proximity, access, and consistency. In this way, we do not always select companions specifically, but our activities determine our fellow pilgrims. When we share similar—or even the same—events or experiences, we create a bond with the others involved. A connection forms, and we share in a very human process that fulfills our need for bonds, companionship, friendship, and fellow travelers. We cherish those who Journey with us because we are invested in the shared endeavor and thus, in each other.

How can I do this, we ask, when I have no energy to give, when I am at my lowest point, when I feel so numb, or even at a negative point? This is a great question. We need to connect to something. We reach out to activities, events, locations, places, and gatherings. Because we are on a Journey, we will meet others who are also Journeyers. We will meet other pilgrims, and the experiences we share will help us balance the ups and downs, and twists and turns of the *Path of Grief.*

I am reminded of a trip I took to Brazil the year my Dad become ill. I met with a Catholic nun who arrived in the Recife area for a six-month assignment, and then stayed for eleven years.

After spending some time with Sis. Allison, she offered to take me with her to her special ministry of outcasts from society in the mangrove swamps. We would visit a camp set up next to a centuries-old church originally built without windows or doors due to a lack of funding. Thereafter, the little church remained "the church without windows or doors" intentionally for easy access to sanctuary. To this day, the lack of a door and glass in the windows remain as a symbol of the tradition of sanctuary, which is still sometimes necessary. The church is a simple one-room construct, barely visible inside the dense mangroves, unless its location is known.

To reach the church required first driving out on the giant reef off the coast of Recife, Brazil after sunset. Standing on the reef, we signaled with a kerosene lantern, and waited for a quiet man with a small rowboat to come alongside the reef. He warned us to be very careful as we jumped down to the boat, for these waters are famously shark infested.

We crouched in the small boat while he rowed over to the shore, directly beneath stairs cut into the bank. The stairs dated to the time of the conquistadores, and were covered in slippery moss. Timing our exit with the rise and fall of the little boat, we flung ourselves upward and outward, grabbing hold of the moss-covered sides of the stairs, and began to climb up and away from the water.

We hiked into the mangrove swamp, led by a guide Sis. Allison knew. We reached the camp and were immediately welcomed.

We shared a dinner of bean soup, and then gathered for mass with refugees and outcasts --our fellow pilgrims-- inside the Church. The outside of the church is non-descript, but the interior walls are layered in vibrant, larger-than-life, expressive, overlapping murals and motifs with the Cross, predominant. We stood, tightly packed together, with barely enough room for the barefoot children to scamper amongst and between adult legs.

Standing at the front, the priest began to speak of Life. He said Life consists of big and little things, all of which make up the Journey. With visible compassion he slowly mentioned how much of the Journey is sour or bitter, and he bit deeply into a cut limón he held in his hand. He gestured to a group of women who came forward and picked up baskets filled with cut lemons and limes to pass around to us, as we stood, listening. I reached in and took my piece of fruit, bit in and sucked the sour juices, absolutely acknowledging the look on the priest's face and those around me as he elaborated on the sadness we experience. He spoke of sickness and disease, of hunger and privation, of violence and war, of abuse, torture, and death. He revealed heartbreak and loss, and with each of these he mentioned specific instances and named names. We in the congregation nodded and some of us cried. Others gasped for breath. Some reached out to hold and be held.

The Father changed his tone of voice and smoothly said, "And yet, amidst the bitter, we also experience the sweet." He bit into a chunk of dark, brown sugar he had pulled out of another basket. Again, baskets were passed around as we each took a chunk of the sticky dark sugar.

I hesitated for a moment, wondering if I could handle so much sweetness at once, but noticed those around me eagerly press the dark sugar to their lips and then quickly push it in their mouths, their eyes glistening while the priest spoke of the reason for the sweetness. He said that we share each other's joys and lift one another during times of trouble.

The woman on my left reached out and grabbed my hand. The man on my right looked directly in my eyes and smiled tenderly as he smoothed the hair of the child resting in his arms.

It was time for communion. Handmade loaves of coarse bread passed around the room, and each of us tore off a piece. A large, metal goblet went from one person to the next as we shared the Blood of Christ with a sip of wine and the Sign of the Cross. I do not know when the singing started, but I joined in eagerly, easily. I stood among fellow travelers—never strangers-- as we felt jointly grateful for life, for being able to stand so closely packed together in solidarity, safety, and peace for that moment in time.

Who will be my friend when I truly need one? Where will I find companions when I alternately have no energy and then other times feel the extremes of emotion uncomfortably grip me? The answer is that I will find friendship and solace from those I stand with or nearby. If I am close enough I will have hands to hold. Life is indeed bitter and sweet; not usually at the same time.

Where can I take myself to be in the presence of others who can help me to balance the extremes and the changes in my Path? The answer is that each choice I make will be a right choice when I am true to my Authentic Self.

- My grief does not mean I am needy for friendship.
- Friends and companions are a necessary aspect of the Path to help balance the burden of sorrow.
- It is entirely ok to choose my friendship circle from amongst the pilgrims on my Path, from various opportunities and choices.
- I do not have to provide ALL the energy: simply balance the load by contributing to/joining the group.

One of my friendship groups might be related to my father's death in some way, as I continue to follow his Path. This might be what I need for now. Maybe extended family members or support groups that share similar stories will be what I need. What have you discovered about the need for friendship and how your contemporaries and companions understand your current *Path of Grief* (or not)?

One of the (if not *The*) most important aspects of a friendship circle is the opportunity to tell our story. The dialogical relationship inherent in pilgrimage that I mentioned above means just that: We tell our stories and we listen to other's stories. And then we do it again. And again.

I tell you my stories, and it reminds you of your own. You tell me your stories, and it reminds me of mine. Counterpoise and equipoise.

In my adult years, contact with my father was mostly over the phone. As he and I discussed and debated human history, we agreed that there is so much more that is glorious and mighty to report from our collective past than the wars and deprivation that yes, must also be admitted.

We often disagreed over the nature and details of what constituted advancement or progress, but we both marveled at the breathtaking innovations representing awesome developments in which individual people employed techniques and skills which were simultaneously correctives and adjustments to the previous innovations and improvements . . . which would cause additional, necessary inventions to counterbalance the weight and pressure of ever increasing splendor.

In other words, as human beings our paths connect, intersect, combine, parallel, and is this not a great thing? We buoy each other up and help to make it possible for one another to continue the Journey. Is it important to understand how each progression and advancement made it possible for the next, or just note the occurrence? Most of all, I think this is about being part of it all.

EQUIPOISE AND COUNTERPOISE: WHICH ONE OR BOTH?

But, but, but . . . is reveling in human achievement that somehow transcends the here and now what I really want to focus on, or is this rather about a desire to reach for more and then go and do? Is that the legacy my father gave me? Am I thinking more about how those many conversations not only shaped our relationship, but also traced the Path that helped define my life's journey? The words we shared resonate within. Past and present combine to offer memories that cause me to ache with the missing of so large a figure in my life. Once we lose someone to death or loss, how do we measure the impact? Maybe that is the wrong question, because measuring implies quantity. I think it remains a notion of balance, because these memories help me recognize my self, and how (when and from where) I have learned to live.

Adding companions to the journey who also recognize that same essential self continues the process of correcting and adjusting: of balancing the Eternal Present. The equipoise and counterpoise continues in ongoing movement.

Movement: that "thing" that occurs in a relationship or community where there is drive and a dynamic. It is something singular and unique–almost indescribable–involving inside jokes; quick smiles, teasing; easy camaraderie; and shared joys and pains. We notice the ups and downs of those with whom we are close —in proximity or otherwise—and sometimes even cause the suffering.

The joint endeavor is partly about pain and suffering, don't you think? Is it because my companions have seen my pain that makes me trust them, or because they smile when I join them and I feel a sense of belonging?

Cicero tells us that in true relationship pain is diminished and joy multiplied because of the process of sharing.[26] This part of the Path, and what I am learning and living through now is a part of that.

As I move along I am learning what my father lived and how he chose the companions on his Path. The *Path of Grief* is a piece of the Journey, and somehow I am in search of my True Self. How I choose companions on the Journey and interact with them is another crucial piece.

Dad, Is it possible for you to have chosen
the legacy you left behind?
Or is that for me to decide?
Is your legacy a part of the process of forming
the Path for me?

How many of these lingering relationships will
form the fabric of the companionships of my
future self?
Is part of the *Path of Grief*, a process of
learning about companionship, now that you are
gone?

Will you and "us" provide a pattern for me?
Is it like this for everyone?

In the Odyssey, Homer writes:

> *Even his griefs are a joy long after to one*
> *that remembers all that he wrought and endured.*[27]

Life seems to consist of a series of balancing acts. . . of
equipoise and counterpoise . . . and the ability to choose.
Perhaps we also need diversions to relieve the tension
or redirect the stress that accumulates. Maybe it is more
than that: perhaps we need to consciously recognize
(choose?) the other pilgrims on our path in order to
venture forth in a way that feels right and true for the
Self?

Like the sculpture my father made, undoubtedly I am a product of many corrections and adjustments along the way. I am thinking (hoping?) that my beautiful friends who make up my friendship circle distribute the weight of the burden I carry, and I hope I sometimes do the same for them.

If I hope to find myself now, after the death of my Father, it will be in a place of belonging where I can water my roots—maybe even establish new roots—and recognize my True, Authentic Self, with people who acknowledge my Journeying Self.

"Deep grief sometimes is almost like a location, a coordinate on a map of time. When you are standing in that forest of sorrow, you cannot imagine that you could ever find your way to a better place. But if someone can assure you that they themselves have stood in that same place, and now have moved on, sometimes this will bring hope."

~Elisabeth Gilbert[28]

Chapter 10: Betwixt & Between

I dare to think about Hope. I began to believe in hope so slowly. I mean, I started to entertain expectations and tap into my beliefs in a way that helped my Path begin to sort itself out—even move in a forward direction. I thought about balance as part of negotiating new aspects of the Path. I actively acknowledge the gratitude I felt as I went (and learned anew as I went).

Clearly, our beliefs have an impact on our thoughts and feelings, and this combination shapes our Path. Identifying and meditating on our beliefs makes for a purposeful Path. Formerly aimless trudging becomes purposeful. I look back at the Path I have trod, and have a better sense of the continuing story that shapes me. Think consciously about your ongoing path and focus on your attitude. How has that shaped this journey?

My father had an adventurous spirit and I have mentioned before that we spent a great deal of time exploring and camping in remote places. On one spelunking expedition, he and I went into an abandoned gold mine in an old ghost town. Besides the pure enjoyment, the motivation was turquoise: he was looking for the underlying color *qua* color and the movement of turquoise in its essence. Of course, gold mines are the best source for rich veins of that semi-precious stone.

We descended into the mineshaft, and it was steep and deep. His instructions were to listen carefully, because the map he held was ambiguous. The rubble under our feet did not allow us to stick close together because of the frequent slipping, but I followed his flashlight and his voice. The recollection of his expression: the hushed tone, the sharp mixed with the soft, beckoning sound when he was in teaching mode ... oh, how I miss that!

We were looking for the chute that would lead us to the lower level. He kept me apprised of the conditions we were encountering, and also why he chose which passages. Sometimes we stopped and he made me choose ––with his guidance–– through a series of questions. Understand now, he was relentless, and there was never any room for wavering or what he called "silly behavior."

That was fine, for I was never a silly child.

We wound through many passages, sometimes quite easily, sometimes making use of the rope, and sometimes narrow and difficult. Eventually we came to a giant cavern. When we stepped through the opening, the sight was one of the most amazing of my life.

What was once a natural cavern had been worked and enlarged by long-ago miners into a multi-story mining extravaganza worthy of Hollywood. For whatever reason and whenever the mine closed, they apparently just walked away, leaving everything in place as if it had only been a few moments before. If I squinted away the dust and grime of the previous century, what lay before me looked just like a movie set.

A wooden ladder stretched across the entire cavern, and my Dad suddenly announced: "I'm going to climb it. I need to see where it leads! Keep your flashlight trained just ahead of me."

My mind said "Noooooooo!!!!" but my voice said "Ok."

I was certain the ladder would crumble into the dust of a hundred years if not in the beginning of his climb, then right about the middle when he was suspended in the air, so tiny that I could not see him as a person, but as a traveling speck in the dark.

I held my flashlight as he directed, but I imagined him falling, and me, dragging him back up through the long passages and chutes, and twists and turns of the cave.

Once again, as he climbed, he kept up a steady stream of reassuring words by telling me what it felt like and what he was thinking as he negotiated a ladder-bridge that swayed more, the further he went. When he said "Keep it steady," I wondered if he was talking to me with the light, to the ladder, or to himself!

He stopped in the middle and shouted, "I'm completely suspended in space, honey, look!" He had no need to tell me; I was already thinking that to myself!

I think back to that moment, and consider myself
in a similar situation:
betwixt and between;
suspended in space;
and neither here nor there.

How do we find a way that is "forward" when
the only goal we know reaches backwards?
Is it "backwards" if we move in a different way
with newfound thoughts and hopes, and then
return to safety to begin again?

My Dad swayed on the impossible ladder in thin air, and then he laughed that glorious laugh of his: the real one, no holds barred. The sound resonated throughout the cavern as if it were made just for acoustics. He disappeared into the dark, and I had only his words to guide the light I held. I worried that it did not reach him, because eventually I could not hear his voice, but only guess.

I wish I had a picture to show, because words fail, but I do not need a physical image for my own memory. It is indelibly imprinted; as is the smile he wore when he came back down:

Pure Satisfaction

Perhaps the process is not about going backwards, but rather about finding a way home. This is not a simple statement, because "home" is a complex notion. Maybe home is more like the idea of home base: a situation and a place that holds my True Self from which I can then venture forth? Home Base remains no matter where we roam or how far. We can go back to Home Base and begin again.

Is this like recovery? When the Self gets scattered or seems suspended, it can take a while to gather up the pieces and place them back together on Home Base. In the meantime, we remain betwixt & between, not knowing for certain, as we sway back and forth, how far we must go until we will return. Then begin again. Maybe the ability to venture forth has more to do with knowing Home Base, than it does with knowing the ultimate goal.

I am reminded of the true meaning of *Confidence*, which is about living with fidelity. Being True to Oneself is the route to confidence. How cool is that? To walk a Confident Path, is to be True to the Self.

When we learn to think purposefully, we will form a purposeful Path. On the other hand, if we think indiscriminately, we will form an indiscriminate path. If we do not pay attention to our thoughts, we will not be paying attention to our Path.

Patience with our Self is required, for the Path is not easy, and it is unique for each of us. The importance of allowing for the True Self to emerge is important, for it happens in an attitude –expectation-- of hope and possibility. Nothing can be forced; the Path is what happens while we, with confidence, venture forth.

One afternoon, I walked out of the History Department Building using the stairwell in which I had spent so many tense afternoons discussing details about my father's last days with Dr. Hodap. At the end of a day's lecturing, I breathed in deeply as I climbed the stairs, loving the feel of freshly washed air from a steady day's worth of rain. I looked up to the blueness of the sky, and my eyes met a spectacular sight: double rainbows splayed across the horizon!

- They welcomed and revived me.
- They beckoned me.
- They felt like Hope.

The rainbows seemed so close; I thought I might just touch them, and I entertained fanciful thoughts as I walked to my car. I imagined I could feel their energy. As I started my car, I decided to follow the rainbows to discover their destination, or would it be their origin?

I drove for an excited twenty minutes, continually getting closer . . . closer. . . until all at once I came to a field on the side of the road where the two vivid arches poured themselves into the grass. I pulled over, jumped out into the field, radiating with joy. I cartwheeled and danced, and soaked up the magic. This, too, became a part of my Path.

No longer betwixt and between, with Hope a reality, I am free to move towards what-is-next.

"The depth of the feeling continued to surprise and threaten me, but each time it hit again and I bore it. . . I would discover that it hadn't washed me away."

~Anne Lamont[29]

Chapter 11: Swept Away

What is Memory?

I have asked this before. Is it a slice of thought residing within the recesses of our minds? If so, where is that and why is it simultaneously so much a part of the Self, but also seemingly outside my/our control?

Here and now in the Present, as I contemplate my True Authentic Self do I remember playing in the water with my Daddy OR do I remember looking at pictures of me, playing with my Daddy in the water. . . recalling family commentary, telling me

- how I felt,
- what I wanted,
- what I understood. . . ?

Could it be all of the above? If memory exists in a stream, moving through a life either along with or as a result of time, then it would be not only the event that makes up who I am (a daughter who played in the ocean with her Daddy), but also a girl and then a woman who recollects remembering the anecdotes and pictures based on the event.

Is that also Memory?

In an "Essay Concerning Human Understanding,"[30] John Locke wrote of the stream of consciousness that makes up a sense of our individual self. He declared Memory a part of that stream, and essential to understanding identity. According to Locke, we negotiate our past and anticipate our future based on the process of remembering.

This relates to seminal events like the death of a loved one, as memory has an impact on grief and then of course, on my Imagined Future. Selfhood is about more than a culmination of the events of my past, arriving at my Present Self. When I rested in my father's arms, or even walked towards him learning to walk, aiming toward the goal of my father's arms, the memory includes the before and after-ness of it, as there is always an objective or a next, and there is more besides, because of course my life is filled with walking alongside my Dad, and just plain ol' walking. Memories do not exist as solitary events, but in context and in a continuum with commentary that is continuously overwritten and multi-layered.

People seem to like to remind me that my father will always be with me in some way, and perhaps this is what they mean.

I cannot separate those layers of memories from the Me-Who-Exists-Today, nor can I undo the understandings I have processed about Myself-and-the-World that have created the Path I have trod. Like learning to walk, once accomplished: one has arrived somewhere, somehow, and in a certain way.

Remembering times with my father is an integral part of what makes me who I am today, and this explains a part of my struggle with his death.

Ready or not and whether or not I am drawing upon a specific activity that sparks a particular and distinct memory, innumerable impressions of being in and near the water flow together in my mind as the most natural habitat for this creature that is me. I look at photographs of Baby-Gabrielle, Girl-Gabrielle, Young- Woman-Gabrielle, and then the Woman-who-is-me, and the satisfaction I felt then, I know now. I nod to myself, knowing of the things I share with him. The ebb & flow; or the rise and sudden dip that is automatic rhythm to a sea child causes a yearning for dark blue water that never leaves the soul.

- Surf
- Sand
- Seagull cries
- Towels
- Buckets & Shovels
- Tide Pools
- Sandcastles
- Kool-Aid
- Sand crabs
- Jellyfish
- Seaweed
- Whale Watching
- Laughter
- Shivering-Cold-Chattering-Teeth
- And always the surf
- And the sand

Even now, I feel the itchy-scratchy residue of sand, alien to my little-girl-skin, which must be washed away.

After...

- After we romp and play.
- After we swim in the ocean,
- And after we cavort like mermaids
- ...there's always the afterwards

122

The sand in the water adheres to our bodies like an additional layer of skin, but it irritates. We cannot ignore its presence, even if we also squeal and squirm when Mom gets out the hose to wash us off before we step inside the house with our sandy bodies and feet!

Worse, when we come home with tar on our feet, and Dad has to scrub it off with a turpentine-soaked rag.

I recall the smell mixed with screaming giggles

. . . and the tortuous bottom-of-the-foot tickling as Dad rubbed and growled: "Hold still so I can get this tar off you!" in his best pirate voice. . . . Dad, you were such an awesome pirate, and never better than when you read *Treasure Island* aloud to us at breakfast. (I cannot meet anyone named Jim without a flashback!)

I am a child making sand castles daringly close to water's edge. This is a game I like to play; a race against the tide / a race against time.

Same thing?

This feeling that I am journeying towards some kind of goal pursues my thoughts. There is this sense of urgency almost, as if I am supposed to finish my grieving and "go" to a next somehow or somewhere.

Like building a sandcastle, will I finish the many turrets with drip-decoration, window'd depressions and multi-storied balconies, tunnels and moats, walls and escape routes— before the tide claims my work? I learn over time that tributaries and estuaries allow the water to trickle into the moat as I try to channel the encroaching tide, with my imaginary princess safe in the highest tower, until finally–WHOOSH!

There's always that one wave that knows no wall, recognizes no moat, and ignores the sandy bulwark.

The castle becomes a dream. . . a memory

. . . swept away.

How often have I stood at water's edge, bracing myself against the pull of the tide, digging my toes into wet sand, sinking deeper, feeling the tickle of sand crabs and imagined sea creatures?

Staring out to sea with one's feet buried, yet also feeling the tug as the water rises, is a form of contemplation. I gaze longingly out and beyond, past the breaking waves to where mermaids, selkies, and seahorses beckon, and I know my thoughts form bridges of discovery, too.

The call of the sea can sweep you away if you are not careful.

I stand on the pier in our hometown, Dad, and I peer out and into a sea of nothingness. I wonder why you left so many times. Why the wanderlust, and was it worth it? With all my heart I hope so, because I missed you every day and I miss you now. The other day I was in your art studio, and I stepped through a doorway and thought I saw you standing there. Your figment did not smile, and I did not say anything. I turned and walked away.

When you were in the hospital, during your very last days, you woke up suddenly, and blurted out my name:

"Yes, Dad, I'm here."

I reached for your hand, and kissed your forehead, as usual, brushing back your thinning hair.

"There are so many people," you said, and you squeezed my hand too tight.
"I know, Dad."
"Too many people," you told me as you shook your head.

"It's ok to let them go," I looked straight into your eyes. "You are a bold man. You can say good bye." I wondered if I had learned how to be brave from you?

"Say good-bye, yes." You nodded. You placed both your hands on mine.

"It's ok to say good-bye to me, too." I smiled at you, and I wondered if I meant it, as you looked deep into my eyes in that particular way you ~~have~~ had. I cried through my smile.

I thought: "If only I could wash away my fears!"

Grief sticks to me unbidden, and I have no metaphorical rag of turpentine to scrub it off. There is no scratchy tickling reminders, and no pirate-voiced Dad, except in my memories, where I find pictures of my self.

Sometimes when I am driving nowhere or just washing dishes, or even sitting still on a solitary park bench, a wave of sadness washes over me without warning, fills up all the empty spaces and carves out new ones.

Melancholy encroaches

It ignores my walls, overflows my reservoirs of strength and topples my defenses. The enormity of your gone-ness carries me away into a different where and when.

Again.

Sometimes it is little things like a street sign in Paris, and thinking about the way YOU pronounce a particular word with your silly antics, and laughing at the thought of the phone call, NO, crying at the phone call that will not happen.

> So I ask again: What is Memory?
> And is it supposed to be this conflicting?
> Is it Layers?
> A Rushing, Roaring Stream?

Do images of life and present day blend to form the idea of the Path experienced with your loved one who now is gone?

I am in Chartres with my beautiful daughter who is so much a part of me but also so much better and more . . . yet my lingering memories stick to me like seashore sand. They scratch at the corners of my mind as I wake up early and tiptoe in to check on her, sleeping.

I am transfixed just watching her, and delight in every moment of her first time in Europe. Her happiness makes my heartstrings grow and glow, and yet . . . and yet. . . Those scratchy places have left empty spaces in my heart.

In *Confessions, Book X,* St. Augustine of Hippo presented Memory as synonymous with the Mind in an active role, and essential to any sense of Identity.[31]

According to Augustine, Memory is the point of departure for reflection and the condition of possibility for all experience, along with understanding and will. This makes Memory crucial and even indispensable.

Reflecting on my childhood, bound up in the grief of your loss, Dad, I am forming the Path upon which I will inevitably venture forth. Possibility beckons, I am certain, even though my feet feel mired in hard, wet sand that pulls me out to a sea of sadness.

According to Augustine, through understanding my past —in whatever way— the possibility of my Future Path is formed on these experiences . . . and is that not always true for each of us? Even as I exist in the Eternal Present, as a product of my Stream of Memories, I can only "go" into a Future I have Imagined in the way I understand my Self.

I have so frequently leaped, face forward. Right now, I seem to be covered in a layer of grief, and I am once again swept away, awash in memories that flood my senses. How can Grief-in-the-Present co-exist with Hope-in-the-Imagined-Future? Can I feel both at one and the same time?

When I tell someone my father died recently, their countenance visibly changes in dramatic ways. Their visage lengthens; they look inside the self somewhere, deep and introspective. Their voice goes soft, and they reach out almost uniformly saying something like,

"There's nothing like that kind of pain. It never goes away, but time makes it better somehow."

They say the words aloud, but they appear to be talking to a private self. They each say they did not expect it to feel the way it felt and that it caught them unaware. I see in their self-awareness --now projected outward—that they were forever changed by the experience.

The death and dying of my father is now a part of the Stream of Memories upon which I am forming the Understanding of Life, which leads to my Everyday-ness and my Future Self.

- So many things to think about
- So much to revel in
- Contemplate
- Discover Anew
- Gaze at the Horizon
- Leap

Get Swept Away

"The reality is that you will grieve forever. You will not 'get over' the loss of a loved one; you will learn to live with it. You will heal and you will rebuild yourself around the loss you have suffered. You will be whole again, but you will never be the same. Nor should you be the same, nor would you want to."

~Elisabeth Kübler -Ross[32]

Chapter 12: On Being Stuck

I think about moving forward, but cannot yet imagine it. At least not right now. I know no direction. The doldrums are like that, y'know, while the ship languishes at sea, waiting for some outside force to nudge the vessel back on course. Previously sailing along at a goodly place with favorable winds, the voyage is suddenly placed on hold.

Wait a minute, how do I know if this is about wind? Sure, I have been stuck in place, or circling in a fixed position, but now that I am thinking about movement, what if this is less about wind (external forces), and more about forgetting to unfurl the sails, or rather, about me, taking some kind of action for my voyage? What if there is no correct direction to fare forward, but movement is what matters and one direction is the same as any other? How will I know when an opportune breeze presents itself and I should take hold, when everywhere I look,

- I am sucked down into the muck of memories
- mired in grief and immobilization
- stalled in stuckedness?

I know about being stuck. Perhaps I even expected it. No, I think this is a way of saying that sometimes the *Path of Grief* feels fatalistic. I think we can confuse destiny with doom, and look at the past as a source of confirmation instead of a resource and a form of contemplation. There are many ways to access our Stream of Memories.

When I was growing up, one of our favorite family camping spots was a place called Afton Canyon. Dad chose it because of a cluster of mesas upon which we discovered obsidian arrowheads while hiking along the connected cap rocks.

As children we loved exploring and playing in the river that ran through the canyon. Once upon a time we rescued a baby opossum in that river, so that discovery somehow made it especially our Personal River!

On one such camping trip when I was about 11 years old, my brother, sister, and I said good-bye to our parents as soon as camp was organized, venturing forth with the family dog, our Irish Setter Fergus. We set off through the brush for about half a mile from camp, and then turned to hop and skip over rocks across the river at our special opossum spot. We hiked for another quarter mile to pass under a rusty iron bridge no longer attached to much of anything, and came to a butte, jutting out, into our path.

We knew what to expect next, and held our breaths in anticipation. We were ready to round the corner to behold a perfect pond ringed with mesquite trees poised to frame a path on the far side of the pond. The three of us remembered the path from the last time we visited, beckoning us to further adventures. We meant to take advantage of that opportunity.

Fergus ran ahead and we followed him eagerly until we came around the corner only to stop short, for our lovely pond was gone! No beautiful clear blue water littered with lily pads met our gaze; no pretty scene framed by mesquite trees; no water at all!

We froze in surprise and dismay.

What happened to our pond, and now what should we do? A full minute went by. And then another.

Young Piper decided that never mind the lack of a picturesque pond, the adventure of a trail waiting on the other side still beckoned three young explorers and their dog. My brother and sister cheered! Fergus ignored us all, and went about doing what dogs do: galumphing about in the bushes in his ungainly stride, sniffing the ground and fallen branches, with his tongue hanging out, happy dog look.

"Wait," I told my sister and brother. "I think we're fine, but it's all caked mud and we don't know what to expect. I'll go first, and you guys follow." So saying, I stepped out, onto the baked, cracks of mud that used to be a pond.

"I think this will work!" I called once halfway across, and then took one step more and my foot was caught. I turned back to my siblings all in one motion, and the other foot joined the first as I yelled: "Stay there!"

I stopped in place. My body lurched as I sunk to my ankles in brown-green slimy mud. My immediate thought was of two choices: ought I remain still as can be, or should I attempt to move immediately, all-at-once, while I still could? If I wanted to move, it likely would best occur right away, so I chose to move.

132

I sunk to my knees instead, though it felt like I was sucked by something real—by a force from below, like concentrated gravity.

My siblings immediately began to look for long sticks or branches; perhaps some other adventurer left behind an old rope? We thought there might be something to toss out to me, the sinking sister, and pull me out. We called to Fergus who was happy to answer, but he did not understand:

"Go back to Camp!" or "Go get Daddy!" and he refused to tread on the mud to rescue his little girl. We commented on all the *Lassie* episodes we had watched, and how "Timmy's in the well" did not seem so different from "Piper is stuck in quick sand!" Apparently Fergus had never watched us watch *Lassie*.

Meanwhile, I had sunk in the green slime up to my thighs while the three of us discussed searching methods and I had experimented with the options:

- Was it possible to lean backwards and move onto the surface? No.
- Could I move a small section of my body to extricate it? No.
- Could I remain absolutely still and halt the downward sucking of my body? No.

I was trapped as if glued in the epoxy Dad used on his wall murals. No part of me could budge, no matter the attempt. I continued to sink. I was stuck up to my hips when we decided Galen, my little brother, would run back to camp: around the cliff, under the bridge, across the fields, over the river, through the brush, and back to the parents at camp. Then bring Dad back to save me.

"Ok," we said.

"Let's pray," I said. They knelt, and I spoke the words. Then I smiled at Galen and said, "On your mark. Get set. Go!" Galen took a giant leap and bounded over a rise, ran three steps, and tripped.

"Hey!" he yelled. Dana ran over, and together they started rolling a log—the log over which he had just tripped!

Somehow they had missed it before, because it looked to be part of a tree, but now, together they rolled and pushed it over the mud and out to me. I was submerged to my waist, but now I knew I would be okay. I could stop thinking about alternative ways to breathe while submerged in quicksand, and how to mark the place where I would have disappeared.

I grabbed hold, and my brother and sister pulled me out. It took their combined concentration and effort, but they never stopped to rest until I was all the way free.

Fergus continued to trample the bushes and sniff for trails, ignoring his children companions.

The disgusting smelling, brown-green slime included dead bugs and rotting things, but I did not care. I did not mind that I could not bend my knees for the gooey thickness and the weight of it on my jeans. I was glad I was free and walking back to camp on my own feet.

We three were silent on our trek, and Dad met us right after the stream as we started walking through the brush, apparently thinking we had been gone too long. He never voiced the question he was going to ask as he stopped, stared for a moment, then reached out, took one of my hands, and looked me up and down.

"Well then," he said. "Let's get you cleaned up."

I remember the look on your face, Dad. I noticed the pause as you chose your words. You swallowed hard, and hesitated. I wanted a hug so badly I stood there in watchful silence wishing buckets of hugs at you with all my 11 year old might. But I was also strong, and I am your daughter. We turned and walked back to camp.

Many years later, when you thought I was in another room, I heard you tell one of your friends, "That's my daughter Piper. I never worry about her. She can handle anything."

You never really knew, did you Dad?

And now I am stuck again. I do not know the way forward. I do not know how to unstuck myself. Perhaps I need rescuers with a plan, or a log to roll out to me. Maybe the story is as simple as I was sinking, and then I was unstuck.

The question is how to become unstuck?

There is no moment during the sinking stillness or the downward pull of grief that is marked with an X as in 'here: this is grief.' This could be followed by a moment in time or out of time which can be marked as "enough already, for I am done with grieving."

I have knelt in silent prayer, and also cried towards heaven countless times. I have repeated words as mantras, and I have executed dozens of heartfelt discourses to the open air. When did I stop praying so often about losing my father, and begin praying to find myself? At some point, it was not so much about my Dad, and not even about loss. It became about the way forward. Now I am the voyager, stuck as I am, in memories and more:

Time present and time past
Are both perhaps present in time future
And time future contained in time past . . .

And it is not over.

You shall not think the past is finished . . .[33]

Daddy, I wonder if I need permission to live in a brand new way. I do not believe I will be following your path, after all. Your destinations will not be mine. Despite the adventuremental mindset, the mermaids and the poetry . . . and I wonder if that is okay? I know how to voyage, after all. I know about the wind and rain, the currents and the waves. I recall how I arrived here, at this place, and how to set my course. I simply need to . . . Go!

I think I will be one who perches more often than you did. I want to know my children, and I want them to know me, so there are no doubts for them about who they are and are not.

But the Adventuremental Life: I learned that all from you. Is that the way our loved ones live on through us?

We shall not cease from exploration
And the end of all our exploring
Will be to arrive where we started
And know the place for the first time.[34]

"No hour is ever eternity, but it has its regret to weep."

~*Zora Neale Thurston*[35]

Chapter 13: Fare Forward, Voyager[36]

When I began this journey of Grief and Loss, I naively thought I would come to some kind of destination: an 'end.' I thought a LOT about time vs. no time, but I did not understand how much I had to learn about the nature of the many ways we as human beings live and move through time even as time continues outside and all around us in various ways.

Partway through my Journey, I traveled to the small town of Anagni, about 45 minutes south of Rome. I went in search of specific mosaics and one fresco panel in particular, but I discovered so much more than I expected. One of these discoveries was a perfectly preserved crypt under the twelfth-century papal palace and cathedral complex that once was the seat of the most powerful men in the western world. Now, in the present, visiting the complex was a lonely exercise not unlike the Path I have traveled in learning how to live with the death of my father.

Anagni is beyond beautiful. The narrow, paved streets wind upward to the impressive Bell Tower and gorgeous Romanesque palace and cathedral at the height of the summit.

The cathedral is fairly simple, yet majestic in the way that fills all the senses at once, then rests inside one's blood vessels and bone marrow as if it has always been there. It has presence and weight that goes well past the massive stones of its walls or the extent of the view to the valley below.

Upon reaching the cathedral and contemplating the immensity of the place along with soaking in waves of splendor that permeate sacred spaces, I slowly opened the small wooden door to enter, and stepped onto exquisitely preserved Cosmati tile floors. Frozen in time for 800 years; reverence and power from the scenario overcame me all at once. At the end of my first day at this site, I would tell people that I had just experienced 'the perfect day.'

Light from the sun's rays poured through stained glass windows and strategically placed cuts in the stone walls. My footsteps echoed with a percussive welcome across the tiles I would later ascertain were the original pieces. I was alone and in a place of wonder. It was up to me to choose whether and if I went further, and therefore, what I might find.

Could that apply to any part [all?] of my Journey?

Being no stranger to cathedral layouts, I turned to the aisles and searched in the shadows for small chapels and hidden stairs. After walking up and down and then up once again, in a narrow nook I found a curving stairwell tucked away in a dark corner. To my surprise, I also heard the faint sounds of a song filtering down the steps. I half wondered if I imagined it. Never mind, I started to climb, slowly, so as to enjoy each moment. The twisting, narrow stairway rose swiftly, and I quickly discerned guitar strings and a tenor's voice. I slowed my ascent, desiring to savor the moment. Eventually I arrived on a landing flooded with sunlight streaming through a large open window void of glass. A young man straddled the windowsill, with his legs half hanging out of the tower, cradling a guitar across his chest while he sang with his eyes closed. He did not turn to look at me as I entered, and I said nothing.

The moment was perfect just as it was: centuries'-old carved stones, tradition, beauty, and two travelers caught in the same moment of time. When he finished the next song, I turned and stepped back, down the stairs.

I spent the entire day at the cathedral until I had no light, and I would spend many more days there as well. On that first day of exploring I found another set of stairs near and behind the altar, leading down to an ancient, beautiful crypt.

In the crypt I discovered painted and preserved for centuries, a medieval notion of Time in its variations, displayed within frescoes of people moving and living in different ways and meanings of Time(s).

I loudly thought "aha!" There are so many ways to think of the Voyage, are there not? I had been waiting to come to the END of a long journey, when in reality, this was about life and I had been living it all along. I carefully studied fresco panels portraying countless scenes of life and death and life vs. death. I felt a bond with people who lived oh-so-long ago, yet they painted my story so well! Grief is part of life and a necessary part at that. Death, too, is part of life, and I had been walking that Path throughout.

- I already knew about the Eternal Present
- And I knew about the Stream of Memories
- I also knew about the Imagined Future

I simply had not put them together in ways that matched daily life. I somehow thought they were separate aspects of the Journey like neat little packages. Spending time in a beautiful cathedral where a boy sang in much the same

140

way that many had sung before, I was grateful to also discover and revel in a beautiful art-filled tomb.

Every surface told a story as meaningful today as when it was painted centuries ago. There before me in layers of limestone and paint were simple depictions of the human condition as naturally existing in different, layered perspectives—depending on context, yet still so similar to my life now.

We live and Journey with others. We die. My aliveness screams defiance at the death and the dying journey of my Father, yet death helps delineate the Journey by giving it definition. My True Self is always and will always BE in the Eternal Present. My Path and The Path relates to moving through time, or maybe Time moves through me? Either way.

Does it Matter?

The death of a loved one seems to stop that movement, but that is simply a snapshot view of The Path in a sliver of time as it relates to my perception. I still exist in the Eternal Present, and I am still on The Path, even if I seem to have paused in my forward movement. The Path consists of everything I do and am. I am a Person who:

- Thinks
- Feels
- Imagines
- Believes
- Acts
- Connects [to Others]
- Reflects/Remembers

. . . and goes through these motions and behaviors continuously.

The Eternal Present is interconnected as we move through these steps of The Path, and none of them require forward movement. My Journey through and within Time includes the Stream of Memories that led to this point.

Without those memories, the sense of loss that I feel would not be so great, because the burden of emptiness—can nothingness also be a burden?—feels so huge! Now, while I exist in the Eternal Present

- I Think deeply;
- I Feel acutely;
- I Imagine beyond;
- I Reflect.

The Imagined Future opens in my mind and a pathway forms. Like finding that half-concealed stairwell in the cathedral at Anagni after feeling the enormity of centuries worth of weighty stone bearing down while simultaneously reaching towards the heavens; then moving about with no map. With a few ideas floating ahead of me, I begin to move in new directions. I think of it as climbing in the dark because it feels difficult and I am new to life without a Dad in the background. In real time in the cathedral, I use the map design of the tile structure of the floors to understand how to view the frescoes on the wall. The more I inhabit the space, the better I understand it.

Grief is like that too. I am not going to move beyond the death of my father; I am learning how to live with it and better understand how to do so all the time. The pain and various poignant thoughts and feelings provide a map from which I learn how to inhabit a world in which my father has passed on, and whose death is now a part of my future path. How about you? What are you learning and what have you discovered along the way that provides a map for you now?

I still occasionally pull out my phone to call him, only to remember that he is not there. I have not yet removed him from my contact list. I wonder if I will? I like to see his name on the screen, and I imagine conversations we will never have.

Sometimes my eyes tear without warning, and I suddenly realize that I am missing him fiercely in a seemingly infinite moment of sadness that is all about daughterness. Lately I have recognized that I will always have this part of missing him deep inside me, or maybe that is just part of growing up. Growing up is an ongoing Journey, and grieving is one of the feelings we are likely to encounter on The Path.

I live and grieve?

No, I do not think so. I believe that I live and now I know better how to grieve. I understand this is a part of My Path. I am ready to discover a Forward Journey.

"I know now that we never get over great losses; we absorb then, and they carve us into different, often kinder, creatures. . . We tell the story to get them back, to capture the traces of footfalls through the snow."

~Gail Caldwell[37]

Chapter 14: The Imagined Future

I began this Journey all in a moment, seemingly aware of the difficulty of capturing a single measure of what we call time, and longing to do so because I felt the weight of it; the searing pain of it; the presence of each instant as it happened. I acknowledged and announced its presence: that capsule of existence that would inevitably pass, but would leave its mark. It remained because my Dad was dying, and I did not know how to mourn.

- Should I focus on my memories?
- Ought I dwell in the eternal present?
- Would I be able to forge a path into the future?

The thinking, feeling, believing, imagining, connecting, acting, remembering path is very human and very much a part of daily life. The memories along that path have brought me to this place and in this way. Now I face another direction, looking forward to the future. Where does the future exist? Since it has not happened yet, it exists in my imagination, and that is truly magnificent!

My Imagined Future is my choice, and it is as true a statement as I have said before, that I can only GO where I can first imagine. My new and ongoing experiences add to what I can (and dare) to imagine.

This journey of mine, and learning to be a daughter whose father is now gone from this world, has been filled with more and different than I could have anticipated. Now, I imagine a portal leading into my Imagined Future.

- How will I get there?
- Is time a factor?
- Will I be the same 'me' when I arrive?
- How much of this Journey do I get to choose?

I have learned that this is MY Story, so it is time to choose the Story I Live. The same is true for you and YOUR story. How do we do that? I imagine my story (My Life as I live it) in the possibility of my Imaginings. Every good story has a Beginning, a Middle, and an End. So, too, our lives, but what rule says there is only one Beginning, one Middle, and one End? What rule determines the order of events? A life filled with meaning will encompass a path that traverses mountains and valleys; twists and bends in unexpected ways that both terrify and delight.

I hope for a meaningful life. This means I can expect variation and even opposition or trials. I hope for a purposeful life, and this is just it: Hope is a great statement to make!

I stated above that the Imagined Future begins with Hope. Like the double rainbows in which I danced, hope is about more than Dreams. Hope is making it real:

- Allowing the self to Desire.
- Staying open to Possibility.
- Outlining and Reaching for Expectations.
- Preparation for the Journey ahead.

Hope is about the Ideal Possibility becoming Reality. We shape Possibility with each step we take. We form Possibility into Reality as we describe it to our self along the way. I whisper to myself these ideas about where I want to go and who I want to be when I get there. I anticipate the way I will feel and expectation builds. I prepare in little ways for a life I believe I can live. Do you do the same?

If our Goal is a Meaningful or Purposeful Life leading to Happiness, then once we have an idea of our goal, we experience Hope: we <u>Desire</u>, <u>Expect</u>, and <u>Prepare</u>. Another way to say this is that we allow for Possibility, and direct ourselves towards it. Hope is part of the Journey.

We could liken this to starting each morning with a Map. This map charts our course in a way that is recognizable to our True Self. It is unrealistic to think we can arrive at a destination irrespective of our beginning point. I cannot travel from here to there without acknowledging that I start from HERE to get to THERE.

If I want to arrive at a desired Imagined Future, I will necessarily need to travel there through the muck and mire, the fog and the desert or lonely places that lie between the Present and Future. I need to be willing to do it. I might need to be Adventuremental! Depending on how I travel, and the map I use (my Expectations and Preparations), I <u>will</u> however, arrive.

I cannot suddenly declare a new beginning as if all that has gone before does not exist: my story is ongoing, and the Path that led me to this point is important. Thank heavens for the magnificent middle of the Journey that is often messy and even scary.

The Mid-point of the Path is supposed to be unresolved. The Path beyond: the Imagined Future beckons, and my goals will determine the way I develop that Path because my Path —even at the mid-point—will point towards the Imagined Future for which I hope.

Hope is exhilarating. Hope is enervating. Hope is a miracle become Possibility. Hope means we know our desires and can therefore chart our expectations and make preparations. Better than that, hope is a signal that we do indeed desire; that numbness no longer has hold of our heart or mind. Hope is an exquisite tingling, growing, effervescent, bubbling sensation living within our deepest self, and we can allow it to grow by owning it Name it. If we do not know —and articulate-- exactly what it is we want, our desires are unlikely to arrive in our lives.

This sounds deceptively simple, but of course it is not. When death and loss touches our lives, it is difficult not only to know what we desire, but also to simply desire. This is perfectly valid. It is normal. It is part of the numbness that descends for a while.

Until we are ready to face the pain and enter into a dialogue with the Self that feels such depths and voids of emotion, we will not be ready to venture forth . . . and that is okay. There is no specific blueprint for the *Path of Grief.*

The map we uncover as we Journey is individual and tailor made. It is based on our situation, our surroundings, and the many facets of our True, Authentic Self.

Moving towards the Imagined Future, we achieve our goals once we know what we Desire, and part of the grieving process is allowing anguish to have a say in the direction of the path that leads to a Meaningful Life. It is purposeful, because we acknowledge the Grieving Process as part of life's journey, and recognize it as a part of our Self, yet we choose to move forward nevertheless. How interesting is this? Hope provides an anchor for the soul. Grief is part of our life, and so is the development of Hope. They go hand in hand even though there is time in-between; time spent in mourning. Without that depth, the anchor of Hope will not be sufficient to anchor us in a reality that makes sense and will provide what we need for purpose and meaning.

Eventually, we

- Desire,
- Expect,
- and Prepare

for good and specific actuality to manifest itself in our life to come. Then we need to

- Experience.

We cannot dictate what that experience will be; we must be ready to live it. We decide to allow experience into our life. We learn what kind of role Grief will have on our Imagined Future, and thus, what impact it has on our Life's Journey. Sometimes it is so difficult to know what [and how] to expect of our selves. Even so, we can be brave AND gentle with our lovely selves as we Journey.

Hope is a beacon. It is a light that provides us with the ability to see the Path when we might think we live only in darkness and sometimes see no end. Hope offers a glimmer of what might be. Hope is a gift.Hope refreshes our mind like a clear breeze or clean spritz of water. With all of this said, it is most important to understand that Hops is a Cause, not an effect. We do not stand still waiting for some occurrence that will invite Hope into our life. We actively practice Hope. Hope is a Cause and it will bring with it all the positive benefits it promises. You will be on your way to the meaningful life that was meant for you: not like fate, but the one that you have earned and yearned for.

> Dad, You made me think I was invincible, because you were always there.
> Until you were not.
> How do our perceptions of the relationship we had with our deceased loved one shape our current path?
> Is this something that can be changed?

And what is a Meaningful Life? This is one of the great secrets of life. Grief is one of the Paths on the Journey that teaches us that True and Meaningful Happiness is hard won. It is not fleeting.

A purposeful Life requires a capacity for depth and nuance. We cannot snap our fingers and demand that Meaning, Purpose, or even Happiness arrive. In fact, this is the essence of mourning: we face death and/or loss and learn to live anyway. This is it at the heart of it all: most of all we have learned to live. It is the Experience of life that matters. This has to do with living and being:

- Open to experience
- To Consciously endure
- Seek Understanding
- Welcome Insight
- Be unafraid of Suffering
- Acknowledge Loss
- Practice Hope Daily

To experience a life of Purpose and Meaning, all steps of the Path lead to an Imagined Future that equals our Idea of a Meaningful Life. Again, this sounds simple, but it is not. This takes thought and ongoing, mindful attention and preparation. It takes the maturity that comes from growth. We cannot gain wisdom by wishing for it.

The experience and perspective we gain during our trial of grief allows us to grow and mature if we let it. Growth and development does not happen without experiencing life. It cannot occur on a leisurely, unenlightened path.

We want to grow and even flourish, so we cannot avoid the pain and suffering that comes with or occasions that growth. When we imagine our surroundings: not so much the specifics, but the attitude that equals the Authentic Self that is 'MeWonderfulMe' and 'YouWonderfulYou' and then is reflected in the world directly around us, then we are close to inhabiting a genuine, authentic place which the Self can recognize.

We do not judge ourselves harshly in the midst of grief, for it is entirely appropriate to mourn at the death of a loved one. It is normal to react to defeat or harm. The length of time we grieve, and how we find The Path to our Imagined Future is uniquely formed by our singular experience, and cannot be dictated by someone outside the Self.

We need to be kind to our Truest Self in the long, dark, aloneness, and the moments of despair. We will be prepared to be similarly kind to others when they meet their overwhelming trials, face their tests of grief, feel too damaged to continue, and pick up their burdens of isolation and mourning. The Imagined Future is real, but it is only available when we —each of us-- are ready to

151

imagine it. The Imagined Future is ideal because it is yours and it fits you. No one else can be a better you than YOU.

My Dad taught me this important lesson. He said I could always chart a Path if I was conscious of my surroundings, and knew where I wanted to go. We talked about this one year while I persistently plied him with ongoing questions about *Alice in Wonderland*, which Gramma Bea had recently read to me aloud. Dad emphasized the lesson of the Cheshire Cat who answers Alice when she asks for directions, and the cat tells her that it depends on where she wants to go (or it does not really matter).

Touchstones

I wear an amethyst ring on my pinky finger my father gave me when I was 12, and also have amethyst earrings my daughter gave me for my birthday just last year.
The pieces of jewelry become touchstones to people I love and have loved, and also mark my path with my birthstone.

The Path did not stop when my father died, and neither did my Stream of Memories. Ongoing memories mark the boundaries of what it is to be me. This is true for you and for all people.

I miss my Dad's hugs a thousand times a thousand, but have children and grandchildren that I have hugged ten thousand time and plan to hug ten thousand time again. Life's Journey continues. How do you mark your Path? Each day creates new memories, which coexist with the Path of Grief. Each moment carries Possibility and the potential for a touchstone that not only marks our boundaries, but also helps us find the way forward.

Who do you see each day or week? Where do you go and what do you do? What kinds of ongoing memories are you creating as you engage in these activities? I go to lunch with colleagues and celebrate with them their moments of triumph. Together we cheer when our favorite Thai restaurant is so successful, that the proprietor is able to expand.

We eat there so often that the owner feels like a friend; he is certainly one of the pilgrims on our shared journey. 'Before' and 'After' blends into what becomes my Journey and it is not only before and after death took hold, but other things as well. I sit and contemplate a starry sky from my backyard, my mind filled with myriad thoughts and imaginings; memories, too, and the night's reverie is added to so many others: then and now, alone and with others, with my Dad alive and not.

I now own and occasionally wear a red cape, and even though it is a touchstone to my youth and evening walks with my Dad, the cape also carries with it comments from friends and strangers: fellow journeyers on my Path. I wear it as I attend a poetry reading with my friend Marie, and we laugh together. I also sit on the floor Indian style at the local bookstore, reading the poetry I shared with my father, and contemplate the Path: The Path of Memories and also what lies ahead.

Over time, the emotions that build and connect with others combine with memories both old and new, providing more touchstones that carry us into the Eternal Present the way we continue to imagine it every day. What we think and how we go about enacting what we believe, and then how we reach out and touch those who share our Path (or allow ourselves to be touched) become the way we envision our Path. It is about action.

One morning, Dad woke me up at dawn: "Time to get up honey, we're going to the woods." I did not question him. I just got up and dressed for adventure in my favorite pink jeans. We drove in the semi-darkness with a sun-and-moon-shared-sky overhead.

"We're going to Los Padres [National Forest]," Dad explained, and then talked to me about Manzanita trees and the unique thrust of the hard wood, the rich texture of blended reds, sometimes bleached to gray; the smooth bark, and the thin but hard wood branches. (My Dad often explained Life in terms of color.) Once we arrived, we exited the Land Rover and entered the forest to begin our task of collecting fallow pieces.

Great granite boulders thrust up from the ground in-between the twisted burgundy-branched trees, and Dad walked forward with me, carefully pointing out distinct characteristics of the Manzanita trees with particular examples along the trail. I took note of the smooth red wood and the stiff, twisty branches forming such incredible, unique outlines against the sky. He told me about their berries loved by bears, and mostly urged me to discover their beauty. Then he left me to wander on my own. We split apart to explore and gather wood, willy-nilly.

"Here is where I'll meet you later," he said. "Look closely at this formation," he directed as he pointed to a group of boulders.

I thought I followed his instructions, because my eyes did the looking, but I considered the path ahead in a generalized way only. Mostly I absorbed wat was directly surrounding me. It was frighteningly beautiful, and thus distracting. At first I had no worries/no fears, because I knew where I stood: at the center of the forest. I looked for trees that matched the descriptions Dad had given me, and soon discovered that every tree matched the descriptors in some detail.

When I decided to find the trail back to Dad, however, I found I had confused depiction for landmark, and now I had no idea where I was or how to move forward. I concentrated on the trees, searching for differences, and instead saw them come alive, their skinny branches turned into arms with claw-like hands and long, bony fingers stretching to the sky. I observed the winding trunks, and imagined blood-red trees bending down and clutching me with their hard-bark claws, capturing me to rot in the forest!

I began to whimper and tell myself that I was lost. I scanned the sky to determine if the trees might be growing taller, blotting out the sun. I was afraid, so I stopped. I acknowledged my fear. What could I do, alone in the woods, searching for landmarks and imagining a fear-filled zone instead? Maybe landmarks are different than touchstones, being determined by something outside the self. What do landmarks matter> What matters is making sure the Path allows for Possibility, and thus is marked with touchstones.
Feeling alone in the Manzanita forest, what could I do? Needing confidence, meant I would reach inside to my Truest Self. Reverence has always been an integral part of who I am.

So I prayed.

On one beautiful sunshiny day when I was six years old I stood inside a small grove of aspen trees in the front yard of my family home and felt "It." The sun poured down through the dappled leaves and bathed my face as I engaged in conversation with Deity. I will forever remember the details of that moment in time.

Thereafter, I would often return for spiritual discourse. Is it only deemed a prayer when we kneel? Kneeling has an important place, but sometimes I have found my deepest prayers occur while standing, face lifted to the sky, like that day in the aspen grove.

Now in the Manzanita Woods it felt natural to stand with my face to the sky and simply talk. I prayed about the beauty surrounding me. I also prayed for the need for clear eyes and thoughts. While I was afraid, my fear diminished me. I became smaller, and less able to move forward, so I reached for a statement that was Strong and True.

I had forgotten to establish my beginning point. These thoughts return to the idea of a home base. I looked at the boulders individually, and touched them with my open hands. I felt their presence like touchstones on the Path.
Step by step, I found my way, I started to hum, and then I found my singing voice. I started with some breathy little vocals, but it worked, because I recognized myself in the sound. Then I sang a little louder. I sang louder still. I thought about the giant boulders that were my touchstone and my goal.

Dad had pointed out to me the position of the sun, so I knew which direction to face. Like the song, if I stayed still, I would remain scared and alone, but if I could just fare forward, I would find my way. I knew the direction to walk between and amongst the boulders and trees, so I walked, and prayed, and sang. Before long, the path appeared quite clearly. Eventually I saw my Dad ahead, leaning against the boulders, waiting for me. Head held high, I sauntered up to him with a smile.

"I liked your song," he told me.

"Thanks," I replied, relieved he had been there all along.

I felt lost, but in reality the scary part was the separation from my Dad.

Is that what death is like, too?

When someone dies or otherwise leaves, the feeling of loss is so very strong and the path so seemingly undiscoverable that we can feel lost even though we are still <u>here</u> and living our lives.

The absence of a person, even a person we were not currently with or with all the time is a void that feels like a missing portion of life's path. Sometimes we lose ourselves.

- How can life's journey continue when part of the path is gone?
- How can I not remain lost when the sameness of the nothingness allows me no landmarks and I do not know the direction to go?

The loss of a loved one causes lost feelings and we imagine lost path scenarios. We search for landmarks, and sometimes we have to

- Tap into our quiet self
- Encourage clear borders and a path to surface,
- Discern the boundaries along our desired path,
- Reach deep inside and pray,
- and then fare forward.

And is this as easy as the words written here? Of course not. Like wandering in a confusing fore with no clear path, but the one we create ourselves, Life's Journey requires every bit of courage, confidence, compassion, and consideration we can give our True Self. Tenderness matters. Sometimes humor is required.

Obstacles

When I was very young our family went on a camping vacation in Yellowstone National Park. Gramma Bee came along.

One night I woke up, needing to go potty, and neither parent wanted to take me. I almost agreed with them because I was afraid of the cavernous concrete facilities with the cold metal toilets.

Then again, I <u>really</u> had to go!

Gramma Bee tsk-tsk'd, put on her sturdy grandma shoes and said, "I'll take the child."

I held her hand as we walked to the concrete block of stalls and metal sinks. She helped me get up on the large toilet, when suddenly we heard a loud clanging noise!

"Oh no! What is that?" I whispered.

"Let's go see," Gramma responded with a gleam in her eye. She lifted me down, and then we tiptoed quietly toward the sound.

What did we see? A tree frog trapped in a toilet, hopping and bopping its head against the hard metal rim, attempting (and failing) to escape. Feeling our presence, the poor frog became frantic, yet nevertheless remained trapped.

First step: catch the frog, and oh, we had such fun! Gramma showed me how to pet its little head, and I was charmed by the way it closed its eyes.

"Can I keep it?"

"What do you think is best?" she asked me.

"I was thinking you would say that," I replied, so we took him outside, and watched him happily hop away.

Next we sat on the ground with our backs against the concrete wall of the facilities, legs straight out in front of us. Gramma Bee told me a story about how a bright little tree frog went exploring in the woods one night and happened to fall into a toilet . . .

Both Gramma Bee and Dad taught me that I always have the power to choose my reaction. She said that everything we encounter gives us an opportunity to reason things out and find a purpose or meaning.

Feeling lost but recognizing the touchstones that lead to home base-- or to what-is-next --is important. We cannot make it happen in any specific time frame, but we can learn how to do it. The first step is identifying— even imagining—a goal, them aiming towards it.

It is okay and even normal to feel turned upside down. Like over-estimating the power or timing of a wave while body surfing, and turning, spinning topsy-turvy, unable to discern which way is up or down inside the mix of water, bubbles, and sand, we can find ourselves gasping for breath, not knowing which way to go, or even stand upright. Grief can be like that, even when we think we have mastered the forward Path.

At the beginning of my Journey when my Dad was dying, I thought my goal was to "move past" the grief somehow. I have discovered instead that part of being human means that I will grieve.

Each of us mourns in our own way and in our own time, but we also have to learn how to grieve and even that it is possible. We lament our loss, and we move forward. We will not be the same. Now we will live our story in a new or different way, as one who has grieved or continues still to mourn, but like the little frog, we can be trapped or stuck in one moment. Then we move on with the experience as part of who we are.

It is okay to grieve because we will understand what we did not perceive before. We will have tender feelings that enrich existence. We will experience compassion and sympathy in a different way.

Sometimes I go for days without feeling sad or even thinking about my Dad. The intervals are longer as time goes by, and I can even feel guilty for NOT actively mourning.

Talking to others about the wretchedness of grief and mourning, I discover I am not alone, so I believe this is part of the process, too. Being people who have now learned to grieve, we will look at life with a new viewpoint. It might not always make sense, but that is okay. If we fully embrace our grief, our Imagined Future will open to endless possibility and Hope.

"Absence is a house so vast that inside you will pass through its walls and hang pictures on the air."
~Pablo Neruda[xxxviii]

Chapter 15: My Father's Socks

It is morning, and I am standing curbside, waiting for the bus. I look down at my boot-clad feet expecting barren ground, and instead take note of thick, colorless grass pressed flat to frozen earth: grass, beaten down in-between snow falls, now exposed during the most recent melting.

I think to myself, "Yes, that is life: crushed and weak, unprotected, and gasping for breath in air too cold to breathe."

I squint against the bleak winter Chicago sun, and continue to stare at the stomped-flat grass. Like one of those optical illusion drawings that show two pictures in one, I no longer see grass, but instead perceive a concentric pattern wherein every tendril is woven into a web that radiates from every other grassy knot. All blades are connected, close-by and/or somewhere in the patch. Knots and shoots become warp & weft, and are securely linked. Trodden by heavy footprints in-between icy snowdrifts, the dreary grass carpet yet lives because of its interconnectedness.

A while later, sitting on the bus, I receive a text from a friend, responding in an ongoing, mostly one-sided conversation from earlier that morning. She writes:

Thx 4 being there 4 me ☺

How often have I texted or vocalized those same words to someone connected to me; someone who listened; someone who cared? And I can listen too, because I am part of the tapestry of beaten down tendrils, gasping the cold winter air and hoping for the breath of life, connected to others who also listen to me.

I think back to the grass at the side of the road. What do I know about patches of grass? I know that eventually, Spring will arrive. It comes every year: not at the same time, and not in the same way or at the same strength, but the calendar moves, nevertheless.

So, too, in life.

We Journey and we are beaten down. Snow falls and ices over, repeatedly. It washes us out and when it melts we can get stomped on. The season passes however, and through it all, we are connected to others who help sustain life. Sometimes we sustain theirs. All that is required is

- Being there
- Showing up
- Listening
- Acknowledging
- Existing
- Journeying

Simple existence can be the same as comfort and warmth in the cold, dark winter times. The Path of Grief does not resolve itself all of a sudden or with some kind of neatly tied bow wrapped around a box that can be placed on a shelf once completed. It becomes a part of life that makes us more complex. We become better people.

Each morning upon waking, I put my father's socks on my feet: feet that are much too small for his wonderfully thick, woolen socks knitted for Maine weather. I love them because they are

- So warm
- So oversized
- And they were his

I take them with me when I travel, and changing into his socks is the first thing I do once I unpack and settle into any new space.

I live in Chicago now, to be nearer to my grown children, and warm socks are also necessary for the winters here. I wear them while I eat breakfast, and I wear them when I read the books that Dad and I both loved, that now my children also read. My feet feel good scrunched inside those socks. All 16 pair—each in different ways.

I thought about keeping your rocking chair, Dad, for there are memories there, to be sure. I considered keeping the model ship of your grandfather's sloop as it brims full with family history. Neither of those compare, however, to your socks. I think about the paths you walked, sure, but mostly, I just remember you. And how I love you.

And I love the me that was and is a part of you.

And the Imagined Future?

I am still considering that. Grieving has been hard. I have experienced the desert and the fog. I know what sinking feels like and also being lost. I have survived the storms and contemplated the Nothingness. I have climbed high and dug deep. I have shared much that could never be duplicated or even passed along, and I have missed you every day since the day you died.

But I missed you before that also, and I figured out how to make that part of Life, so I will learn this too. Now it is time to continue, Faring Forward as the Journeyer you taught me to be. I think I am ready, but not like I thought I would be. That is how it always has been, though, has it not?

When I was a little girl and you raced yachts to Ensenada, you often brought back hand-carved marionettes as gifts. They were so much fun, and the little shows we produced were/are also part of the memory. So too, was your cantankerous pirate voice exclaiming over how many times I brought you a tangled-up puppet to unravel.

(You never were a mumbler, were you?)

I think that real-life, intentional movement is similar to those puppets. It is not so much about manipulating the strings, but whether and if we can keep from getting tangled up. There is a difference, too, between tangled-upedness and life or movement that comes from the woven tapestry of interconnectedness.

When it is time, and when I nudge my mind and limbs, my inner self remembers how to move. Thank you for life's lessons. So many wrapped inside the memories. Past and present connected. The future beckons.

Thank you for being MY Dad. I love you oh so much.

165

Basic Steps on the Path of Grief

- Revel in your Stream of Memories and share them
- Cry
- Follow Rituals & Customs
- Consciously Initiate Customs & Traditions
- Identify your Feelings
- Choose Companions for your Path
- Recognize or Establish a 'Home Base'
- Allow for Possibility
- Learn & Begin to Hope
- Be open to Active Experience
- Imagine the Future

Exercises: Advanced Steps on the Path

Take part in these exercises as you feel ready, and when they apply to you. The exercises are included here in sync with the chapters that discuss each aspect. Feel free to participate for your own best interest.

FOR CHAPTER 1

At Delphi in Ancient Greece, travelers from all over the world would traveled to receive answers to their most pressing questions and even issues likely to rend whole countries asunder. Frequently overlooked by those very same visitors, was the admonishment inscribed over the entryway, which was also almost always the best answer to life's troubles:

Know Thy Self

Who am I NOW?

If and when you feel able, write the answers to the following questions in a journal, and date them. (These answers are likely to evolve as you travel the *Path of Grief*.) It is completely up to you whether or not you share these exercises with anyone else. They are YOUR thoughts and feelings, which gives you the freedom to be completely honest and sincere. This is an authentic exploration of the True Self, with no expectations attached.

- What roles do I play, both private & public? (for example, child, sibling, spouse, parent, other family member, employer/employee, neighbor, homeowner, renter, athlete, gamer, crafter, quilter, bowler, enthusiast, community member, friend, club member, etc.)
- List 5 friends
- Has your list of friends changed recently, with the onset of Grief in my life?
- What are 5 characteristics or attributes that others use to describe me? (See list of attributes in the appendices.)
- What are 5 characteristics or attributes that I use to describe myself?
- Is this list of attributes different now that tragedy and grief have struck—have I changed?
- List (or circle) all of the attributes that describe me.

Objects as Memory Holders

Is there anything I can hold in a pocket, place on a shelf, hang on a wall, wear on my body, or otherwise keep as a reminder that helps me keep the essence of what I miss, now that death or loss has entered my life?

Is there an object that can remind me of good times, of the person who once was, of an event or occurrence that brings a smile or a sense of calm to my spirit self?

Identify it and place it in your daily life.

If I were to ask you about a positive, defining "theme" of your life up 'till now, what would you say—especially if I asked you to give me an immediate answer? Is there an object, a picture, or an image of this theme or idea that you can place somewhere/somehow close by? Is there a way you can evoke the sights, sounds, smells, and feel of this force in your life?

Find it and place it in your daily life, or meditate specifically about this idea.

Identify a Theme

A running theme or overarching ideology can be very powerful in dictating our individual path. A first step in this direction is to determine a Theme Song.

Do you have a personal theme song? There is no "right" answer as to what is your theme song. The important thing is that it is a match to you and your inner self.

Take some time to think about this….to discover or re-discover your theme song and make it your very own.

What is a theme song? A theme song is that tune that plays in your head when you're walking down the street by yourself; when you are afraid and need cheering up; when you stop listening and there's that 'sound' in the background. More: a theme song plays in your mind when you want to calm yourself and be still; it plays when you sit in silence and grow your safe space. A theme song is

- Happy;
- and Sad;
- Dramatic;
- and Ordinary.

It can have words, or be instrumental. It can be any musical genre. When you sit in silence, you will not play or sing the song aloud, but rather, in your mind—deep inside, resonating inside yourself. Eventually, it will become automatic.

Unfinished Business

Using the <u>List of Attributes</u> in Appendix 1, list (or circle) all the positive characteristics and attributes you know about and even love about your loved one.

Using the List of Attributes in Appendix 1 list (or circle in a different color) all the negative characteristics and attributes you know about and perhaps dislike about your loved one

Remember, people are complex, and the True Authentic Self of any person is a multifaceted pattern of attributes, characteristics, actions, and life events.

How many of these attributes are part of a larger story? Do these lists remind you of stories from your shared paths?

Your hard boundaries are physical and evident to everyone. They are visible and detectable by all the senses. Stand up with your feet apart and throw your arms in the air—YAY!

Place your arms on your hips for self power—YAY!

Even on your worst days, you are the very best YouWonderfulYou in the whole wide world. No one else can be a better YOU, than you.

Take care of yourself: eat healthy without extremes; drink water; get a physical & follow your doctor's advice; enjoy the outdoors daily; breathe deeply; avoid negative naysayers; make decisions with care; practice self-care; look in the mirror with tenderness and love.

Touch the top of your head and wiggle your toes. Roll your hips and laugh out loud.

Repeat.

Memories

Gather photos, memorabilia, mementos, certificates, or anything that speaks to you of your loved one and place them together in a way that has meaning.

- Scrapbook
- Slideshow
- Shadowbox
- Large envelope
- Giant pile on a table
- . . . . there is no right or wrong way.

The point is to gather the visible memories, and spend time with them.

Maybe they can be used at a funeral or memorial service, or
maybe they are best for an intimate circle of loved ones for reminiscing.

Maybe they are just for you.

What do I miss?

In my grieving, do I miss only what I experienced and knew of, or do I grieve for what I also never knew and never knew about?

Can it be both?

Write about it.

Borders & Boundaries: (Shared Borders)

List (in your Journal) the shared borders of your Journey with your loved one who has passed on:

Familial: _____ ...
Friendship: _____ ...
Companionship: _____ ...
Shared Friends: _____ ...
Pets: _____ ...
Hobbies or Activities: _____ ...
Religious Expression: _____ ...
Length of time: _____ ...
Shared Location(s): _____ ...
Shared Education: _____ ...
Shared Profession: _____ ...
Shared Experiences: _____ ...
Shared Jokes: _____ ...
Shared Beliefs: _____ ...
Shared Secrets: _____ ...
Hope for the Future: _____ ...
Anything Else: _____ ...

Things left unsaid: _____ ...
Things let undone: _____ ...
Plans made: _____ ...
Hopes: _____ ...
Dreams: _____ ...
Wishes: _____ ...

Borders & Boundaries: (Thoughts & Feelings)

What do you <u>think</u> about death?

How do you <u>feel</u> about death?

What do you <u>imagine</u> regarding death?

Do you share these thoughts/feelings with anyone?

Are these questions too difficult?

Can these questions wait for later? (Yes)

Tradition

What rituals have you noticed within your memories or developed in your family or friendship that you would like to keep or carry on?

What traditions exist in your family or culture that you would like to keep or use to help in your *Path of Grief*?

What formulas have you found that have helped, that you would like to record, so you don't forget?

What do you want to remember most about the funeral or memorial service of your loved one?

Write a letter

Write a letter to your dear, loved one who is dying or who has already died. Do not worry about grammar or punctuation. Instead, simply write from your heart, and say what you most desire to say in your own words.

Date the letter, and place it in an envelope.
Place the envelope in your journal.

Repeat this process each month for as long as

you want.

Ringing the Bell

Make a list of ways that you might establish a memorial or a commemoration of the passing of your loved one. Is this a solitary action, or is it something others can participate in with you?

- Join a support group
- Build a Shrine or Monument
- Hold a memorial, and even make it an annual tradition
- Light a special candle on the anniversary
- Make a special scrapbook or a digital memory book
- Build a website dedicated to your loved one
- Establish a scholarship in the name of your loved one
- Donate to a charity in the name of your loved one
- Write a poem
- Ring a Bell (and keep the bell on display)
- Something else

Borders & Boundaries: (Friends & Companions)

List the friends and/or companions who are closest to you.

Do they listen and understand your thoughts and feelings about your grief?

Do you feel comfortable articulating your thoughts and/or feelings of pain and loss to those who surround you?

Have you met the friends & companions of your departed love one?

Have you heard the stories of these others?

Did your loved one die too soon, without friends, or before there was time to establish long-term relationships?

How much do you want to include these friends (those you know and those you have recently met) in your mourning?

Grounding

Grounding exercises are a way to firmly "ground" the Self in the present, particularly when uncomfortable memories or emotions take hold. This list is in no way exhaustive.

- Breathe in slowly through your nose (count to 7). Hold your breath (count to 4). Breathe out slowly through your mouth (count to 8).
- One at a time, access your senses: What can you see? Make a conscious mental note of it. What can you hear? Can you hear anything else? What else? Mentally add it to what you hear. What can you smell? Can you name the smells? Mentally add them to what you see and hear.
- If you are sitting feel the chair under you and the weight of your body and legs pressing down onto it.
- If you are lying down, feel the contact between your head, your body and your legs, as they touch the surface you are lying on.
- Look around you, notice what is in front of you and to each side, name first any large objects and then smaller ones.

- Place both feet firmly on the ground.
- Listen to soothing music.
- Focus on a particular voice or <u>neutral</u> conversation.
- Identify a grounding object you can keep with you. Any object that comforts you or that helps you stay "in the moment," can be a grounding object. Some examples are:

- A smooth, stone that you have found.
- A bell that, when you ring it, has a soothing sound.
- A piece of sandpaper with a course texture.
- A photograph of a beautiful scene.
- A small vial of a pleasant fragrance or essential oils.
- A piece of jewelry, like a ring or bracelet.
- You may want to hold, look at, smell, listen or otherwise focus on your grounding object. If your grounding object I small enough, you can carry it with you wherever you go. A grounding object can offer access to calm and comfort.
- Trace your hands against the physical outline of your body. Experience your own presence in the world.

Meditation: Sitting in Silence

Every morning, 6 days/week, sit for 10 minutes. You might have to get up extra early. You might already get up extra early, so now it will be extra, extra early. So be it. It's worth it.

Sit still and breathe. Breathe in and out. It's ok to think about breathing. Try to clear your mind, and focus on your garden or cave/pond or stream/flames or fire that you are growing.

Grow (not build: GROW) a safe place that only you know about and only you know how to reach. If mundane thoughts or daily worries intrude, don't worry or stress. Simply shoo them out of your mind like sweeping dandelions gently out the door. "Shoo, thoughts . . . I'll think about you later, but right now I'm focusing on my special place, and simply breathing."

This is about finding yourself. One of the ways you will know you have begun is when you don't need to affirm yourself with others. You will not need to talk to everyone, but only to those who are True and Faithful Companions, and you will choose them. You don't belong to anyone else; only yourself. Your affirmation doesn't rest in anyone else's eyes or hands; only your own.

Practically speaking: spending this extra 10 minutes that you might think you do not have will give you back HOURS in your day and week of productivity, effectiveness, clarity, and insight.

One of the benefits of meditation is the connection we gain to our inner self. It's a process of letting go, and this means letting go of past concepts of the self--even if only momentarily. We want to see our self as we exist in this moment, not as we think others think about us, or how we might exist in a version of the past.... How can we do this? First find your element; discover if you are earth, fire, or water. I'm not talking about something weird or esoteric, but about visualization.

I'll give you my personal example: I have mentioned many times that I am a water person, so when I meditate I focus on water, and I have spent several years growing a beautiful [imaginary] pond. When I meditate, I like to visualize myself as a blue heron, standing tall in my beautiful blue pond. I'm not always the heron, though. Sometimes I'm an otter or a duck, and sometimes I imagine I'm the water lilies scattered about the pond's surface. At times I'm a dragon fly flitting over the lily pads. When I spend my 10 minutes sitting in silence, I am also the pond itself. The water pushes up against the banks, and I make sure the sludge is cleared off. The waterfall that feeds the water keeps it fresh. Sometimes I swim under the water, and sometimes I just stand. It doesn't matter; I draw the water up through my being, thinking about nothing but **being**. And **stillness**.

I have two good friends--one of whom is earth and the other is fire. My earth-friend mediates on gardens and digging: imagining the dirt in her hands.

Sometimes she IS the dirt, and sometimes she is an entire cave or simply a head of lettuce or an earthworm. My fire friend contemplates on burning flames and they feel purifying and powerful to her. (She walks through walls of fire in her mind the way I walk through waterfalls and stand in fountains.) Sometimes she is the tiny flame of a candle or the spark of a match. She smells and tastes fire.

Which one of these images "speaks" to you?

Either in your journal or on a separate piece of paper, draw a quick, stick figure of  yourself. This will be the old self/former self. Think about who/what you are —your attributes. Looking at the list from the former exercise, draw your stick-figure-you, thinking of the attributes you listed and imbue the stick figure with them. Now, take the piece of paper and . . . burn that piece of paper if you're fire, bury it if you're earth, and submerge/drown it if you're water!!!!

You can do this figuratively, or you can do it for real.

In none of these instances will you completely rid yourself of her. That's because YOU are HER, right? You can be grateful for the pieces of her that led you here NOW. Those are precious pieces of self.

Those pieces are the ashes if you're fire, the mulch leftover if you're dirt, and the filtered mush if you're water--always a part of you but not defining. They are not GONE, but neither are they essential.

This is about new beginnings.
It's also about defining the self,
And about boundaries.

Now, draw your stick body self again. Look at the Attribute List (Appendix) and THIS time write,  underline, or circle those characteristics that define you or that describe you, that you want to keep. Identify in a different color or somehow in a different way those attributes you would like to develop (and don't yet have).

A path is made of slight adjustments over time, and now you will meet yourself as you Journey anew.

If you are Earth, when you meditate, think of this as growing the new you in your garden. If you are water, when you meditate, think of this as growing the new formed in water. If you are fire, when you meditate, you can grow the new parts of yourself in flames. Depending on which you are, this makes sense to you in that element.

Keep your drawing or your list in your journal, and look at it occasionally.

Know Thy Self

- Thoughts
- Conscious
- Subconscious
- Unconscious

- Feelings
- Recognized
- Unidentified
- Changing

- Beliefs
- Religious doctrine
- Truth/truth

- Ideas
- Doubts
- Heroes
- Action
- Active/Passive

- Environment/Location
- Lived
- Traveled

- Education
- Research
- Work/Career/Vocation

- Imagination
- Future
- Fun

- Connections
- Friends
- Family
- Companions
- People who have influenced me
- People I have influenced

- Reflecting
- Memories

The Imagined Future: Setting & Achieving Goals Amidst Difficulty

Write down a goal.

If it is easier to think of it as a wish or a dream, that's ok, too.

Write it down on a piece of paper, or better: in your journal.

On the left side of your paper [in your journal]

Place a dot and write • Present

On the right side of your paper [in your journal]

Place a dot for your Goal and give it a name: • GOAL

Here is the crucial part of reaching any Goal:

Backwards Planning

Look at the dot and the GOAL on the right side. Imagine it as reality.

It doesn't matter what this goal is, right now in this moment: imagine your GOAL as absolute reality. For that GOAL to be reality, what other conditions, parameters, events, procedures and processes would also have to be in place?

Why do we move backwards in planning our goals? This is a practical matter.

When we stand in the Present and look forward to a GOAL, the steps involved can seem overwhelming.

If we Imagine the GOAL, instead, and move backwards towards the PRESENT, it is much easier to determine what needs to be done.

Here are two examples: 1 large and 1 small:

Example Goal 1 (large): <u>Finish college degree</u>
   Moving backwards:
   - Graduate
   - Fill out paperwork for graduation and file on time.
   - Complete coursework and requirements for your major.
   - Fill out application paperwork and registration forms.
   - Pay fees.
   - Figure out how long this will take and place it on a calendar.
   - Choose major, or determine best major based on previous coursework or desired work outcome.
   - Investigate college choices and look at course catalogues of each. Evaluate the differences based on your circumstances.
   - Think about the type of college and location of college choices. Make a list of potential colleges.
   - Fill out all paperwork for financial aid.

- Figure out how you will meet the financial obligation, including how long it will take.
- Investigate financial requirements and financial aid deadlines.
- Talk to anyone necessary for agreement with plan/goal.

Example Goal 2 (small): <u>Become a Pet Owner</u>
    Moving backwards:
- Bring home your new pet.
- Buy food and any other requirements for your chosen pet.
- Make arrangements to pick up pet.
- Choose where you will buy (obtain) pet.
- Gain permission from anyone necessary: Landlord; Room-mate, City license
- Investigate types/breeds, and choose.

<u>Next Step</u>:

Look at each item on the list, and decide if it [each item] is a single step, or whether it needs to be broken down, depending on circumstances. If so, then do that next.

Example Goal 2b: <u>Become a Pet Owner</u>
    Start at the bottom of the list:
- Bring home your new pet.
- Purchase a pet carrier
- Make home ready for pet
- Buy food and any other requirements for your chosen pet.
- Food, Bowls for food, Collar? Leash? Cage? Sleeping pad? Perch? Tank? Toys?
- Make a budget
- Make arrangements to pick up pet.
- Paperwork
- Phone calls

- Choose where you will buy (obtain) pet.
- Internet search
- Word of mouth recommendations
- Breeders
- Will you have to travel?
- Gain permission from anyone necessary: Landlord; Room-mate, City license
- Investigate types/breeds, and choose.
- What are you looking for? (comfort, companionship; protection, pleasure, etc.)

Timing

Now look at your revised list. Look at each item individually, and estimate approximately how long it will take to complete each item. Write that time next to each item. Some items will take only 1 day or less. Others might take several years.

There is no value judgment on how short or long something takes. It simply is what it is.

Avoid the temptation of thinking the only goals you can reach are those that are immediate or short term.

Break it down

Now it's time to break down your Timeline into a TASK LIST. You will do this by listing your tasks into five (5)

<u>Task Categories</u>:

1. Phone calls,
2. Contacts needed,
3. To get/To buy,
4. To do,
5. To Research or find out.

Looking at your TASK LIST, is there anything else you need to add to your TIMELINE? For instance, while you are brainstorming your TASK LIST, it might occur to you, in thinking about Contacts, that you need to know someone in a field that you do not yet know, so you will then add a list of steps to your timeline that will help you find that Contact.

Now that you have a TIMELINE and a TASK LIST, you know your starting point (PRESENT) and you know an approximate date for your GOAL.

<u>How to Begin</u>

Like the old adage about eating an elephant one bite at a time, you will walk the Path to your GOAL one step at a time, by giving yourself three (3) tasks. That's right. Assign yourself <u>three tasks only</u> from the TASK LIST. Give yourself three assignments starting at the PRESENT point, (the bottom of the list) that move you towards your goal. Your rule is that you may not assign yourself more tasks until you complete the first three.

Good Moments going Forward

In the midst of pain and suffering, it can be difficult to notice the small, sometimes insignificant but "nice" and good things that occur on a daily basis.

Some of these items or sensations can be purposefully "discovered."

Turn these into active memories.

- Hold and smell puppies/a puppy.
- Watch children play.
- Hang your laundry outside, then enjoy the smell and feel.
- Walk through and sit in a garden.
- Visit a butterfly house.
- Take a community class (art, woodwork, jewelry making, dance, etc.)
- Attend a concert, recital, poetry reading, etc.
- If hugs make you feel good, then find someone to hug
- Walk barefoot through clean sand or lush grass.
- Climb a tree.
- Feed ducks.
- Participate in an enjoyable activity or Join a Meet-up Group: book review, knitting, quilting, bird-watching, embroidery, travel club, etc. (www.meetup.com)

- Take a course in something interesting (www.udemy.com)
- Cultivate a garden.
- Visit an art gallery.
- Go for a walk.
- Make your own list of activities.

Contemplation

What if I said: Writing is Freedom!? I say it now, and I say it emphatically because I believe it so vehemently. Putting pen or pencil to paper and just letting go allows the connection between the fingers and the mind to operate freely, and puts us in contact with a creative force deep inside ourselves even as it unlocks our potential. We are freed. We find hidden sources of strength and talent, just waiting to be discovered. Freedom Writing is a tool that begins the process of love: we learn to love ourselves in all our own individual (wonderful) quirkiness as we lay it all bare on the page.

How to: Every morning before work and before talking to anyone . . . sit down and write. Put your pen/pencil in your hand and write three pages with utter abandon. Three pages without thinking. That's right: stream of consciousness. Write whatever comes to mind. This is not the place for grammar rules. This is not a journal like you are used to thinking about. You are not going to pass these pages on to your posterity. If there is any chance these pages will be read by others, then throw them away (after you write them). You don't show these to anyone—not even yourself! The point of the writing, is the writing process—not what you say. You want to just write as fast as you can think and get the "junk" out of your head and on to the page.

Then. . . If you have the time and the inclination, you can switch and write in a "real" journal. But first, LIBERATE yourself by practicing Freedom. I would no more start my day without this practice, than . . . breathe.

What do you write? Whatever comes to mind. If you hear the birds singing outside, then write that down. If something is annoying, you: write it down even as you think it. If you don't know what to write, then write THAT down. The point is to write, and it will "happen." You will free your inner creative juices, and if you do every day, you will find an inner sense of clarity and freedom through this process. (Yes, it's a form of written meditation.) You will be amazed what comes out of your pen from your newly freeing/freed mind! I promise you.

Freedom Writing

- Re-establishes individual self worth
- Fosters an honest self-appraisal
- Provides an avenue for new interests and ideas
- Relieves emotional/mental stress
- Demonstrates that problems are not new & that there is more than one solution to a problem
- Helps plan constructive courses of action in problem solving
- Promotes a sense of well being

A Conversation

Imagine you can take a walk with your lost loved one.
Where will you go?
Will you hold hands?
Walk side-by-side?
Will one of you carry the other?
Will one of you lead the way?
Jog?
Climb?
Find a place to sit down?
Something else?

Let's say you want to have a conversation, even if you
have been silent with everyone else.
What will you talk about?
Will you ask questions?
Will you ask for explanations?
Will you discuss or argue?
Will you smile and listen?
Will you sing?
Will you hold each other?
Something else?

APPENDIX I

List of Attributes

abandoned
abashed
aberrant
abhorrent
abiding
abject
ablaze
able
abnormal
aboriginal
abrasive
abrupt
absent
absorbing
abstracted
absurd
abusive
acceptable
accessible
accountable
accurate
acidic
adamant
adaptable
addicted
adorable
adventurous
advocacy-minded
afraid
aggressive
agonizing
agreeable
alcoholic
alert
alive
alluring
aloof
amazing
ambitious

amusing
angry
animated
annoying
anxious
apathetic
arrogant
ashamed
average
aware
awful
babbling
bad
baffling
ballistic
barbarous
bashful
bawdy
beautiful
befuddled
bellicose
belligerent
beneficent
bent
berserk
bewildered
billowy
bitter
bizarre
black-and-white
bland
bloody
blunt
blushing
boiling
boisterous
bold
boorish
bored

boring
bouncy
brainy
brash
brave
brawny
breakable
breathtaking
breezy
bright
brilliant
broken
bubbly
burly
bustling
busy
cagey
calculating
callous
calm
candid
canny
capable
capricious
captive
careful
careless
caring
casual
cautious
cerebral
certain
changeable
charitable
charming
chatty
cheap
cheerful
chic
childlike
childish
chilly
chivalrous
circumspect

civil
clammy
classy
clean
clever
cloistered
clumsy
coherent
cold
colorful
combative
comfortable
committed
common
complex
communicator
community-minded
compassionate
competent
competitive
complex
concerned
confident
confused
considerate
content
cool
cooperative
coordinated
cordial
courageous
courteous
cowardly
coy
crabby
crazy
creative
credible
creepy
critical
crooked
cruel
cuddly
cultured

curious
curvy
cute
cynical
daffy
dainty
damaged
damaging
dangerous
dapper
dark
dashing
dazzling
dead
deadpan
debonair
deceitful
decisive
decorous
deep
defeated
defective
defiant
delicate
delightful
demonic
demure
delirious
dependable
dependent
depressed
deranged
desirable
determined
devilish
didactic
difficult
diligent
diplomatic
dirty
disagreeable
diverse
disastrous
discreet
disgusting

disillusioned
disturbed
domineering
drab
draconian
dramatic
dreamy
dreary
dry
dull
dynamic
dysfunctional
eager
early
earnest
easy
easygoing
ebullient
eccentric
economical
edgy
educated
effeminate
efficient
elderly
electric
elegant
elfin
elite
eloquent
embarrassed
eminent
empowered
empowering
empty
enchanted
enchanting
encouraging
energetic
engaging
entertaining
enthusiastic
equable
erratic
ethereal

evanescent
exceptional
exciting
exotic
expensive
explosive
extravagant
exuberant
exultant
fabulous
fair
faithful
false
famous
fanatical
fanciful
fancy
fascinating
fastidious
fearful
fearless
feeble
feminine
ferocious
fertile
festive
fierce
filthy
finicky
flagrant
flaky
flamboyant
flashy
flippant
flirtatious
flowery
fluffy
fluttering
follower
foolish
forgetful
forgiving
frail
fragile

frantic
free
fresh
fretful
friendly
frightened
frightening
frivolous
fumbling
funny
furtive
gabby
gallant
garrulous
gaudy
gaunt
generous
genial
gentle
genuine
giddy
gifted
glamorous
glib
gloomy
glossy
godly
good
goofy
gorgeous
graceful
gracious
grandiose
grave
greasy
great
greedy
gregarious
grieving
grouchy
grubby
grumpy
guarded
guileless

gullible
half-hearted
handsome
handy
hapless
happy
hardboiled
hard-working
hardy
harmless
harsh
hateful
healthy
hearty
heavy
helpful
helpless
heroic
hesitant
hilarious
hollow
honest
honorable
hopeful
hospitable
humble
humdrum
humorous
hurried
hurt
hypnotic
hysterical
icy
ideal
ignorant
ill
ill-fated
ill-informed
illustrious
imaginary
imaginative
immaculate
impartial
impassive
impeccable

impolite
impulsive
inclusive
industrious
infallible
influential
ingenious
innocent
inquisitive
insidious
insightful
instinctive
integrity
intelligent
intense
interested
interesting
intrepid
intuitive
inventive
investigative
inviting
irksome
irresistible
irritating
itchy
jaded
jaunty
jazzy
jealous
jittery
jocular
jolly
jovial
joyful
joyous
jubilant
judicious
jumbled
jumpy
just
juvenile
keen
kind
kindhearted

kindly
kinky
knowing
knowledgeable
kooky
lackadaisical
languid
lanky
late
laughable
lavish
leader
learned
lewd
likeable
literate
little
lively
lonely
longsuffering
loose
lopsided
loquacious
loud
lovable
loved
lovely
loving
loyal
lucky
lyrical
macho
maddening
magical
magnetic
magnificent
majestic
malicious
maniacal
marvelous
masculine
masterful
materialistic
maternal
mature

mean
measly
meek
melancholy
mellow
melodic
merciful
messy
mighty
mild
mindful
mindless
mischievous
modern
muddled
mundane
murky
mute
mysterious
naive
nappy
narrow
nasty
natural
naughty
neat
nebulous
needy
neighborly
nervous
nice
nifty
nimble
noble
noisy
nonchalant
nostalgic
nosy
nutty
obedient
objective
obscure
obsequious
observant
obsessive

obstinate
odd
offbeat
old-fashioned
omniscient
open
opinionated
opportunistic
ordered
otherworldly
outgoing
outrageous
outspoken
outstanding
overconfident
overjoyed
overt
pale
paltry
panicky
paranoid
parsimonious
passionate
passive
patient
peaceful
peculiar
penitent
pensive
perceptive
perky
permissive
persuasive
pert
pervasive
petite
phobic
pious
pithy
photogenic
placid
plain
playful
pleasant
pliable

plucky
poised
polite
political
poor
popular
positive
possessive
powerful
practical
pragmatic
precise
precocious
predictable
prejudiced
prepared
pretty
prickly
prim
pristine
private
productive
proficient
profuse
progressive
prominent
proper
prosperous
protective
proud
prude
prudent
public
puritanical
purposeful
pushy
puzzled
puzzling
quaint
quick
quiet
quirky
quixotic
quizzical
radiant

radical
ragged
rainy
rambunctious
rapid
rare
raspy
rational
realistic
reasonable
reassuring
rebel
rebellious
receptive
reflective
refreshing
relaxed
relentless
reliable
religious
reluctant
remarkable
reminiscent
repentant
repulsive
resolute
resourceful
respectable
respectful
responsible
reverent
righteous
rigid
rigorous
robust
romantic
rough
rowdy
ruddy
rugged
rustic
ruthless
sad
sagacious
salty

sane
sardonic
sassy
saucy
scared
scary
scatter-brained
scattered
scholastic
scientific
scintillating
scornful
scrawny
secretive
secure
sedate
seductive
seemly
selective
self-effacing
selfish
sensible
sentimental
serene
serious
sharp
shapely
shiny
shivering
shocking
short
shrewd
shrill
shy
sick
silent
silly
sincere
skeptical
skillful
sleepy
sloppy
slow
sly
smart

smiling
smooth
snazzy
sneaky
sociable
soft
solicitous
solid
solitary
somber
sophisticated
sore
sour
sparkling
spicy
spiffy
spirited
spiritual
spiteful
spontaneous
spooky
spotless
sprightly
soulful
squeamish
stable
stalwart
stately
staunch
steadfast
steady
steep
stereotyped
stern
stiff
stingy
stormy
straight
straightforward
strange
stressed
strict
striking
strong
stubborn

studious
stunning
sturdy
stylish
suave
subdued
submissive
subservient
subtle
successful
succinct
sudden
suitable
sulky
sultry
superstitious
supportive
susceptible
susceptive
suspicious
svelte
swanky
sweet
sympathy
tacit
taciturn
tactful
talented
talkative
tall
tame
tan
tardy
team member
team worker
tearful
tenacious
tender
tense
tenuous
terse
testy
thankful
thirsty
thorough

thoughtful
thrifty
tidy
tight
tipsy
tired
tireless
tolerant
tough
traditional
transparent
tricky
troubled
truthful
truculent
trusting
trustworthy
tough
unaccountable
unbiased
unconventional
uncovered
undaunted
understanding
understood
undesirable
unequal
unequaled
unerring
uneven
unhealthy
uninterested
unique
united
unkempt
unobtrusive
unorthodox
unpredictable
unpretentious
unruffled
unruly
unsightly
unsuitable
untidy
unusual

unwritten
unyielding
upbeat
uppity
upset
uptight
urbane
useful
useless
vacuous
vagabond
vague
vain
valiant
valuable
various
vast
venerable
vengeful
venomous
versatile
vibrant
victorious
vigilant
vigorous
violent
virile
virtuous
vivacious
vocal
vociferous
voiceless
volatile
voracious
vulgar
vulnerable
wacky
waiting
wakeful
wan
wandering
wanting
wanton
warlike
warm

warm-hearted
wary
wasteful
watchful
watery
wayward
weak
wealthy
weary
wee
weird
well-balanced
well-behaved
wellborn
well-bred
well-connected
well-dressed
well-groomed
well-grounded
well-known
well-mannered
well-placed
well-read
well-spoken
well-to-do
whimsical
whispering

wide-eyed
wiggly
wild
willful
willing
willowy
wily
windy
winsome
wiry
wise
wishful
wistful
witty
woeful
wondrous
worker
worldly
worthy
wry
yielding
young
youthful
yummy
zany
zealous
zestful

About the Author

Dr. Piper Winifred grew up surrounded by stories and storytellers. Her earliest memories consist of long walks with a Dad who was forever reciting poetry and tales of wonder, and of telling tales passed down through generations that always began with, "Once upon a time, there was a little girl named Piper. . ." This book is a product of the journal she kept during and after the death of that father whose life still seems so present sometimes and at others, leaves such a vacancy.

Blending an active imagination and ongoing desire to reach towards identity and authenticity in order to write, this book became the bridge leading to the Imagined Future.

Piper works to discover the authentic origins and elements of stories paired with a rigorous program of classical and ancient languages, archival research, exploration in dusty, musty places: along with arduous translation, and exacting theoretical standards. Understanding the human condition in context has been a lifelong endeavor and academic pursuit encompassing the role of Identity Consciousness and the joy of Storytelling. Her hope is that you will enjoy celebrating life seen through very human eyes thinking of your very own precious Life, and engage in the Journey.

Extracts, References, and Paraphrasing:

[1] Victoria Alexander, www.imaginej.org.

[2] Colin Murray Parkes, and Robert Weiss, *Recovery from Bereavement*, 1983.

[3] Grace Noll Crowell, *Let Me Come In Friend*, Infants Remembered in Silence, Inc., 2009.

[4] Winnie the Pooh, A.A. Milne.

[5]http://www.siskiyous.edu/class/engl12/folksong/john.html

[6] Woody Guthrie Publications, Inc. & TRO-Ludlow Music, Inc. (BMI), Copyright 1940 (renewed), 1950 (renewed), 1951 (renewed).

[7] Sarah Dressen, *The Truth About Forever, 2004.*

[8] T.S. Eliot, paraphrase *from The Love Song of J. Alfred Prufrock*, Amereon, Ltd. 2002.

[9] T.S. Eliot, paraphrase from *The Love Song of J. Alfred Prufrock*, Amereon, Ltd. 2002.

[10] Aeschylus, The Oresteia,: Agamemnon, W.B. Stanford, Editor; Robert Fagles, translator, Penguin Classics, 1984.

[11] T.S. Eliot, paraphrase from *The Love Song of J. Alfred Prufrock*, Amereon, Ltd. 2002.

[12] T.S. Eliot, paraphrase from *The Love Song of J. Alfred Prufrock*, Amereon, Ltd. 2002.

[13] T.S. Eliot, paraphrase from *The Love Song of J. Alfred Prufrock*, Amereon, Ltd. 2002.

[14] T.S. Eliot, paraphrase from The Love Song of J. Alfred Prufrock, Amereon, Ltd. 2002.

[15] Robert McCloskey, *Blueberries for Sal,*

[16] Nursery rhyme

[17] Lewis Carroll, *Jabberwocky and Other Nonsense: Collected Poems*, Penguin Classics, (repr.) 2012. Throughout

[18] Shakespeare, *Macbeth* IV.3.

[19] Shakespeare, *King Henry VI*, VI.3.

[20] Carl Sandburg, "Fog," Louis Untermeyer, editor, *Modern American Poetry*, 1919.

[21] Michael Leunig, *Prayer Tree*, 1992.

[22] Æsop (6th ce. BCE). *Fables*, retold by Joseph Jacobs. Vol. XVII, Part 1. *The Harvard Classics*. New York: P.F. Collier & Son, 1909–14.

[23] Ralph Waldo Emerson, "The Bell," VI. *Poems of Youth and Early Manhood (1823–1834), Vol. IX The Complete Works.* 1904.

[24] Tom Attig, *The Heart of Grief*, 2012.

[25] Richard Bach, *Illusions: The Adventures of a Reluctant Messiah*, Delta (repr) 2012.

[26] Cicero, *Die Amicitia*, paraphrase, http://archive.org/stream/deamicitiatransl00ciceuoft/deamicitiatransl00ciceuoft_djvu.txt, October 17, 2014.

[27] Homer, *The Odyssey*, translated by Robert Fagles, Edited by Bernard Knox, Penguin Classics, 1997.

[28] Elizabeth Gilbert, *Eat, Pray, Love*, 2006.

[29] Anne Lamont, *Traveling Mercies*, 1999.

[30] John Locke, "An Essay Concerning Human Understanding," http://www2.hn.psu.edu/faculty/jmanis/locke/humanund.pdf, November 1, 2014.

[31] St. Augustine, Confessions, Book X, http://www.sacred-texts.com/chr/augconf/aug10.htm, November 1, 2014.

[32] Elisabeth Kübler –Ross, On Grief and Grieving: Finding the Meaning of Grief Through the Five Stages of Loss, 2007.

[33] T. S. Eliot, "Burnt Norton," *The Four Quartets,* Mariner Books, 1968.

[34] T.S. Eliot, "Little Gidding," *The Four Quartets*, Mariner Books, 1968.

[35] Zora Neale Thurston, *Their Eyes Were Watching God*, 1937.

[36] T.S. Eliot, "Dry Salvages," Paraphrase. *The Four Quartets*, Mariner Books, 1968.

[37] *Gail Caldwell*, Let's Take the Long Way Home, 2010.

[xxxviii] Pablo Neruda, *Twenty Love Poems and a Song of Despair*, 2006.

Made in the USA
Lexington, KY
06 May 2017